STEVEN BRIGINSHAW
THE PROFITS
PRINCIPLES™

R=THINK PRESS

What Others Are Saying About This Book...

'To me, Steve, the word 'book' is an understatement. This is a how-to living, breathing manual to create an extraordinary business.'
Paul Dunn, TEDx speaker and Chairman, B1G1: Business for Good

'This book was an easy and enjoyable read. It covers sensible and time-tested ideas presented in a logical format. It's a solid and understated read covering several concepts that are normally not placed side by side. Perfect for a six-figure revenue business that wants to lay the foundations for seven figures.'
Daniel Priestley, Entrepreneur and best-selling author of three business books.

'The PROFITS Principles in this book are packed full of incredibly simple, practical and powerful ideas. Essential reading for every business owner.'
Steve Pipe, Bestselling author and UK Entrepreneur of the Year

'This is an action-oriented book which helps you get clarity to create a life of your dreams. Whether it is through goal-setting, understanding numbers or identifying your path towards profit, this book has a wealth of knowledge specifically for those who have their own business. You'll find practical tips, insights on a winning mindset and interesting experiences that the author shares, most of which resonate with your business journey. I recommend this book to anyone who wishes to accelerate in business.'
Darshana Ubl, Entrepreneur and Advisor

'I've known Steven for a while and I am so excited that he has finally taken the plunge and delivered what is clearly a very well thought through, practical methodology of how to get yourself ready to have the business you truly desire. I fundamentally believe that when you take this book seriously and you commit to doing what is suggested, the only way is UP, UP, UP. The journey is interesting and in the process you will learn far more about yourself and what you can achieve when you have the right tools.'
Elvira Villarini, Transformational Coach

'A simple, clear book packed with tips to take you and your business to the next level!'
Eloise Ansell

'To create a profitable business and a balanced lifestyle this book is *the* book to help. A great how-to guide to profit! I thought the book was going to give me a clear road map from where I am with my job now to owning a sustainable business. I think it does that really, really well and I honestly think it is a manual for every small business owner! Wonderful!'
Adam Cox, Holistic Wellness Coach

I dedicate this book to those people throughout the world who think differently and don't fit within the status quo but instead break through it to pursue their passion.

To those who make a difference, no matter how big, to others on this miraculous and beautiful planet on which we live.

I hope this book brings you the confidence, support and encouragement that you already have what it takes to do what you love and make an impact.

Free download bonuses

Thank you in advance for reading my book. To express my gratitude I want to give you something back that will help you move your business towards your dream lifestyle passion business.

Throughout the book there are references to special free downloadable templates, tips and help that will guide you through your business journey and help you work on the exercises and content in each chapter.

To get this extra help please visit www.stevenbriginshaw.com/profitsbonus.

I really appreciate you taking the time to read my book.

Thank you and enjoy!

CONTENTS

INTRODUCTION

I will never forget that night... I was sitting on the stairs with my little sister in the early hours of morning looking through the gaps of the smooth, white glossed banister. It was the noise of the doorbell during the quiet of the night that woke us and the reason why we were watching from our lofty perch with a clear view of the room below. Even though we didn't speak to one another we both knew something was wrong. And then we were ordered to our rooms to go back to bed by our mum who had floods of tears streaming down her face. At this point we both started to cry too. As the obedient four – and two-year olds that we were, we climbed the stairs and went back to sleep still unsure of what was going on.

It wasn't until the morning that we were told the two police officers who had disturbed our peaceful sleep the night before were the bearers of the bad news that our dad had died. He had died in a vehicle accident while on a night shift for the roadside assistance company for which he worked. He had just helped a stricken driver get home with their broken vehicle and he too was on his way home when the accident occurred. Now it all made sense but I didn't want to have this knowledge. I just wanted my dad to come home.

For a very long time I wasn't able to discuss this with anyone; it was too raw and too personal I would just get teary-eyed thinking about my dad. It wasn't until my late twenties that I found the courage to work with a professional to help me put aside my anger, fear, sadness and guilt so I can remember the times of love, happiness and joy. It was at this point that I understood those negative emotions were holding me back, blurring my vision and obstructing my ability to embrace life. I felt released to fulfil why I am here on this earth and started to notice what I loved to do and what I wanted to do to make a difference.

For a long time I had felt like I didn't belong and that I had failed somehow in life and in business. I put too much pressure on myself to fulfil my potential leading to more mistakes. I felt like I had lost my way and didn't know where to turn: frozen stiff, too scared to take a step in any direction in the fear of not fulfilling my potential, letting people down, not making a difference and getting to my destination too late to enjoy it.

I realised that I would always feel like this if I didn't embrace my authentic self and start to enjoy the journey rather than rush through and be disappointed with the end destination. Life is a journey and one I can choose to enjoy or not. The end destination may seem like life will be great when it arrives but life is great now if you choose to look for the happiness, gratitude and the connections you have. Being my authentic self has made me happy and allowed me to feel like I do belong in this world to help those people who get what I do and what I believe in. Embracing the journey of life has enabled me to see the highs and lows as another opportunity to experience and enjoy myself knowing that the end goal is not the be all and end all.

Knowing that life is short, far too short, I wanted to make the most of my life and enjoy it so I started my own business to explore what I love and ultimately help others do the same.

Without all of the things that have occurred in my life I wouldn't be the person that I am today. In a way I am grateful for everything that has happened, good and bad, and I honestly believe that those things have happened for a reason. I do every day miss my dad but I now think of and remember the wonderful time we had together in those short four years of our father-son relationship.

All of my learning and experience up to now have helped me to develop The **PROFITS** Principles™ that I guide you through in this book. You will find the seven steps that you need to follow and revisit, as often as you need, to build your dream business and create your definition of success.

As a Chartered Accountant I get to see hundreds of businesses with their clothes off – I see their numbers – regardless of the image and brand they might have I know what's really going on. Lots of these businesses are not performing as they should partly due to the numbers not being looked at or being understood and partly due to the owner not doing what they should be doing as an owner. Numbers are the language of business but it's scary that so many people either don't know, don't like or don't understand their numbers. Sometimes all three. I'm their reality check because they may have been putting their head in the sand or putting on a good show and I can tell them how it really is and what to do about it to get to where they want to be. I'm able to help them understand their numbers and then help them to take a step towards their goals.

Throughout my career I have noticed that far too many business owners do not fulfil their potential and far too many businesses do not achieve the impact that the owners set out to achieve. This is due to a knowledge gap in business and entrepreneurship because most of the schools do not teach us about this and, with society in general, they tend to push people into becoming an employee rather than an employer.

I also noticed that so many business owners work far too many more hours than they want and often on the things that will not help progress towards their goals. Many do not get paid from their businesses the amounts they want and deserve, some less than minimum wage when you consider the hours they work. The trouble is that most don't own a business; they own a job. This means when they stop working so does the business, and the money stops coming in.

I have been working with business owners and their numbers since 2000. I love numbers and I am fascinated with everything about business, so I put to use that passion, along with my skill as a Chartered Accountant, to help entrepreneurs all over the world build their dream business around their own passions and goals. I've gained valuable experience and honed my skills through my own entrepreneurial journey and learned a lot of lessons from my mistakes; mistakes that, with this book, you don't need to make.

I have also had some recognition too for my work over the past few years. My business won Best New Business in the Best Business Awards in 2013, was a finalist in the prestigious AVN Firm of the Year awards in our first year in business and I won third place in the Thames Valley Entrepreneur of the Year Award.

I'm fortunate that friends and most of the people I know throughout my career so far are successful business people, who have either sold their business or still run a very profitable enterprise. I've helped and learnt from a lot of them. I've had regular dinners with a successful millionaire entrepreneur, who was also a football club owner and chairman, and enjoyed an amazing stay at his hotel. There have been drinks and Yorkshire wrap dinners at the pub with a successful internet start up entrepreneur and lunch with national property tycoons. A visit to my friends' completely rebuilt mansion, who happen to be millionaire internet entrepreneurs, was inspiring. It was also inspiring to get a tour of the island of Jersey while I visited the home of my successful entrepreneur friend and his family. I'm very grateful for these connections and opportunities to learn from some amazing people.

I grew my first real business from zero to a six figure valuation in two years and then sold the business because I fell out of love with it. I now have other businesses, that have been profitable from day one, that I am passionate about, and which are making a real difference to the entrepreneurs we work with.

In my first business, one of my favourite and most proud successes was increasing the average price a client invested in our services by over 131% in less than two years. This was done through knowing my customers, creating a service they wanted, systemising and pricing it correctly, which included a minimum monthly price. This was a game changer for my business and my life.

You'll read about a case study where within two years I helped a client increase sales by 123% to £2.2m, increased their gross profit by 292% and increased their net profit 3043%; that's not a typo – it's mind blowing, right? Another case study shows where within one year sales increased by 22% to over £1m, gross profit increased by 50% and net profit increased by 124%.

In each case study the business owner has gone from working late nights and weekends to leaving the office early and having more time for family, travel and hobbies. The key ingredients for this success were understanding the numbers, planning, focused hard work, systemisation and being themselves. Ingredients you will pick up from this book.

They also had me to hold them accountable and support them in the great work they were doing.

I wrote this book to share my message and to help entrepreneurs find the path to their dreams while trying to limit the exposure to pitfalls along the way.

I believe I am here on Earth to have fun, learn, create, educate and inspire that in others. My journey leading to this book has been about me having fun while learning about myself, others and business; creating products, services and tools, from my own experiences, to educate and support entrepreneurs all over the world as they work towards the creation and running of extraordinary businesses, doing what they love, helping the people they enjoy being with, and living the life they've dreamed of.

Whether you have a start-up and you want to hit the ground running from day one giving your business the best possible chance for success, or a mature business that has got stuck or plateaued and can't seem to get to the next level; the same steps apply. You may find it uncomfortable at first as the focus is on you and your responsibility for your business. You may even find the early chapters a little 'fluffy' but these are essential to make your life more enjoyable and to get you to where you want to be much quicker, before applying the less 'fluffy' chapters afterwards, that make it all happen.

This book is meant to be a companion in your entire business journey. A reliable friend to help you take the next step towards your dreams. A manual to refer to as your situation changes. Turn to specific chapters that are relevant to your current position again and again as your business journey progresses and adapts to change and as you develop as a person and entrepreneur.

Many of the ideas in this book you will have seen before but this is because they work and are tried and tested ways to succeed. Sometimes the search for something new or original can hold you back and distract you from the simple things that really work. Why spend time, energy and money on reinventing the wheel when it is already available to you and may just need tweaking to your situation.

Also the ideas in this book are not normally seen side by side in one place. It's a bringing together of principles, values, beliefs, attitudes, strategy, planning, measurements, systemisation and tax planning. This book is at the intersection of purpose and profit. The key ingredients to getting paid well, doing what you love and building an extraordinary business around it that can stand the test of time.

Trust the process and stick with the book. It will challenge you, but if you do stick with it you will experience success like you never have before.

The world is yours. You just have to grab it.

GPS SATNAV FOR YOUR BUSINESS

A GPS SatNav is the right tool to use on a car journey. You will no doubt know how a SatNav works but let's break it down. You enter where you want to go and the SatNav calculates where you currently are, and suggests the best routes. You choose the route that best fits you, then follow the instructions as you drive. You end up at your chosen destination at the time you wanted and in one piece.

The **PROFITS** Principles are like SatNav for your business. They help you understand where your business currently is; you decide where you want to be and how your business will look – the process helps you create a path from your chosen destination back to where you are today. You choose what to work on each day that best fits your goals and then follow the process as you drive your business. You end up at your chosen destination at the time you wanted and in one piece. But also with a great business with great customers, a great team and great profits to give you the cash and time for the life you dreamed about. Everyone profits from your business!

In other words, if you follow this process and implement the action steps along the way, you will have a profitable business that can run without you, which means you will have the personal income and time to live how you want to live. Not only that, you will be able to sell your business for so much more – or pass it on to your family who will be able to simply follow the systems to obtain the same results and lead to a greater enrichment of their lives.

To create a valuable and sellable business you need profit. To turn your hard work into the cash you deserve and to accomplish your dreams and goals, you need profit. To get your time back so that you can spend it as you see fit rather than being a slave to your business, you need profit.

To be, do or have any of the things you want in life you need the right amount of profit from the business. Not your turnover, your profit.

7

THE PROFITS PRINCIPLES

Your sales don't mean anything unless they are making you a profit.

But here's the thing, profit is just a result, a number. It is the consequence, the end result, of your actions in the business. Get your actions right and you will have profit by the truck load. Get your actions wrong and you will have to put more and more money into the business and then close it down because no profit is made, in fact losses will pile up. You are responsible for these actions and so you are responsible for the results.

By adding seven letters together the end result is the word **PROFITS**. The same principle applies to your business.

Work on each of the seven steps and the end result in your business will be huge **PROFITS**, but it doesn't stop there. You will have the ability to choose how you spend your time and have the money to make your dreams and goals a reality.

Your team will be inspired to work in your business and go the extra mile.

Your customers will be delighted and tell everyone about your business.

You will have fun, energy, focus and motivation every day.

Profits are simply the outcome of what you did before. But you won't focus on the end result and leave everything else to chance, you focus on doing the right things and the end result will just happen.

It happens as a consequence.

A consequence of getting seven letters lined up is a word that has meaning. A consequence of working on the right things in your life and in your business is life changing results for everyone that your business touches. A very powerful consequence that is cyclical creating a virtuous circle with each step building on the momentum and benefit from the previous one.

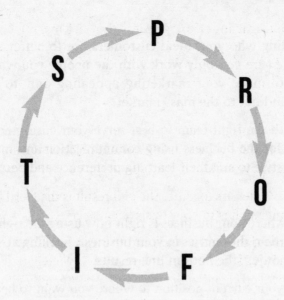

The right actions include, in order:

Plan

Planning for what you want to be, do and have. Turning your dreams and goals into reality with motivation and taking action.

Planning for what your business must look like to achieve this. Linking your goals to the numbers in your business with an understanding of what roles are required and which role you will fulfil. And identifying what your ideal endgame is for your business.

Realise

Understanding who you need to be to run your dream business and potentially the new mindset you will need to adopt to become that person.

Understanding why you do what you do in business and why you started it in the first place.

Realising your authentic self and true potential to make a difference in the way that resonates with you.

THE PROFITS PRINCIPLES

Optimise

Understanding who your ideal customers are to better serve them and to make sure you only work with the people you want to work with. And to make your marketing appealing only to your ideal customers and not to the mass market.

Working with the right team to best serve your customers and fulfil your vision for the business using communication and management in the right style to suit their learning preference and personality.

Focus

Measuring where your business is right now using the right tools and identifying the right metrics in your business. Looking at your whole business – not just the bottom line results.

Comparing your current position to where you want to be.

Improve

Improving your business to move it towards your ideal future with external accountability as your secret weapon. Improving in the three main areas of; profit, cash and time.

Tax

Saving tax, paying the legal minimum of tax that meets your tax morality and saving for tax to have the funds available as taxes become due. Timing is everything.

Systemise

Systemising your business so it's easy for others to follow and get the same great results each and every time. Reviewing and updating each step in the process on a regular basis to make sure you are still on the right track to your definition of success and continuing to make profit just happen.

As you are the business owner these steps should be the most important things you do each day. In fact, they should be the only things you do. Some tasks in each step can be delegated but you need to own this process in your business.

The **PROFITS** Principles are cyclical because life and business are constantly moving. Throughout your entrepreneurial journey to keep moving in the right direction you will need to revisit your plans, your why, team, customers, measurements, improvements, tax position and systems. Also, as you revisit the principles you will see things differently than you did the time before or learn something new because you have also changed.

It may not be possible currently to solely focus on these steps and delegate everything else, but your aim should be to make that a reality. By following the steps you will then build the profits, cash and time to train and delegate the other tasks to your team freeing up even more of your time, making even more profits and having even more cash.

If you love and are good at doing something else in your business like the technical work or the selling you can employ a CEO to follow the seven steps, but you will still need to have input with the CEO to get the right results. So initially you will need to follow the seven steps to get the right message in place and you may need to build the business before bringing in a CEO if you don't immediately have the profits to pay them.

You don't need a 100 page business plan that you will never turn to again. You need this process. This process is your business plan.

This book will take you on a journey showing you how to create profit as a consequence of doing the right things in your business. In other words profit will simply just happen in your business because you are working on the right things. You will have more fun, have more cash and have more time to fulfil your dreams and goals. You will be able to really make a difference to everyone who comes in to contact with your business.

UNDERSTAND WHERE YOU WANT TO BE
Have a dream

When you were a young child you would dream about the future. What job you would have, the car you would drive, the house you would live in and what you would look like. Sadly as you get older those dreams became hazy as they are knocked out of you first through school, through working for someone else and finally, and ironically, working for yourself.

You started your business for a reason but very quickly found out that owning and running a business is not as rewarding as you had hoped. You get stuck working when you had hoped to spend time with your family and friends, which keeps happening more frequently, so you start losing touch with your friends, and your family don't seem to understand why you are not spending time with them.

The money from your business doesn't arrive in the bucket loads that you were expecting so you have to work even harder to try to get the extra cash that you need to provide the things you want for you and your family.

You simply don't feel you have the time to dream.

That is why you need to start dreaming again. And dreaming big.

When you have dreams they become part of your purpose in life. Your dreams are the start of a process that will give you laser-sharp focus on your end result and the motivation you need to achieve it.

In a nutshell, a dream is something that you want to do, be or have in the future where there are no limits and no restrictions on you making it happen. A dream will excite you; it may also scare you. It will help you define what you want to achieve in life.

By dreaming big it gives you a distinct advantage over most other people, they dream small. Instead of dreaming about five weeks of annual leave per year from your business, dream about having blocks of five weeks off five times a year.

Instead of dreaming about becoming the number one business at what you do in your city, dream about becoming the number one business in the world.

Instead of dreaming about helping good causes close to your heart through donation of your time and money, dream about setting up your own foundation to directly help the causes you believe in.

EXERCISE

You may find some of the questions below helpful to get you tuned into your dreams:
- *If you had a magic wand that could do anything instantly, what would you use it for?*
- *What do you want to be known for?*
- *If you had all the time in the world, what would you do?*
- *If you had all the money in the world, what would you have?*

Dream maps

Dream maps are essential to get your dreams out of your head and into the real world. They become real things that can be worked towards rather than one day dreams when one day never comes.

Many successful sports stars and teams visualise their ideal future. They imagine what their future will look like, what sounds they will hear and how they will feel.

Rory McIlroy, the major, multi-winning golfer, will visualise his next shot before taking it. The England rugby team, that won the 2003 Rugby World Cup, would visualise the next match before playing it. The dream map is a step towards you visualising your ideal future. Use your dream map every day and visualise what it would be like to be, do or have all of those things in your life.

It's best to be as specific and vivid as possible as it sharpens your senses and makes the dream feel even more real. If a dream is to own your dream house, for example, you may imagine it to be a symmetrical, new build, six bedroom, Georgian-style manor house, with two beautiful white columns, one either side of the front porch. Inside will be a large kitchen/diner for entertaining and parties, a cinema and music studio room, a gym and a study in addition to a lounge and family room. The simple gardens will be well maintained with three hectares of land around the house so you are not overlooked and surrounded by nature. There is a 100 metre driveway that goes into a semicircle when approaching the house, which also goes up to the separate two storey annex.

There are two rules to a dream map:

1. Your dreams can be anything, do not limit them. They can be as fantastical as you desire. Dream BIG!

2. No one can pass judgement on your dreams, not even you. So don't limit yourself. They are dreams, things that you would like to be, do or have in the future if anything were possible.

Depending on your learning and creative preference you will want to create your dream map in a way suited to your preferred style. Your dream map could be a vision map if you are a visual person, a sound map if you are an auditory person or a mood map if you are a kinaesthetic person. It doesn't matter what preference you have, the process is essentially the same. Collect information about your dreams, what you want to be, do and have and display it in a way to suit your preferred learning and creative style.

Vision Map
Creating a vision map is simply a collection of images that relate to your dreams. You can create a collage of pictures cut out from magazines and stuck together, use Pinterest or use simple software on your computer to create an electronic collage of images that you got from the internet.

For example you may want to be a business owner with financial freedom so you will use a picture that represents this for you. You may want to go to a specific place in the world so you will use a picture of your dream destination. You may want to live in your dream home so you will use a picture of it.

Sound Map

A sound map is a collection of sounds that represent your dreams. You may want to include these as separate tracks or a compilation on your mobile phone and on your computer so you can listen to them every day.

You can find sounds online or have some fun and make them yourself on your mobile phone voice recorder.

For example for your dream house where you will be frequently entertaining all of your friends and family, you can use a sound that means this to you, like background party noise or people singing around the piano.

Mood Map

A mood map is similar to a vision map but also includes text and pieces of objects such as fabric: materials that represent your feelings associated with your dreams.

For example, for your dream house you may include pieces of the wood used in the kitchen which, when you see and touch it, will remind you of the feeling you will have about hosting great parties in that kitchen.

EXERCISE

To get you started, choose two dreams for each of what you want to be, do and have, and write them down below. For example you may dream about being a New York Times bestselling author, or seeing the curvature of Earth from space, or having a billion dollar charitable foundation to help less fortunate people all over the world, like the Bill and Melinda Gates Foundation.
- *Who do you want to be?*
- *What do you want to do?*
- *What do you want to have?*

The answers to the questions are to help you get started. Now spend a few hours on this to expand your list and add them to your dreams map. Have fun doing it.

Once your dream map is complete make sure you put it somewhere where you can see, listen to or touch every day to remind you of what you are working towards. This could be on a notice board, in front of your computer screen or next to your bed. Keep your dream map up to date when you think of new dreams and fulfil existing dreams.

Your life's milestones

Working towards a dream and goal is a journey with lots of small steps to take. It's a bit like running the Great Wall of China marathon. To get to the end and achieve your goal you need to take one small step at a time and although the small steps seem insignificant at the time, when you add them all up they will achieve your goal.

Along the up and down journey to the end of the Great Wall of China you will see milestone markers to let you know how far you have come and that you are going in the right direction. This is also important to have for your own life.

If your dream map is a collage of your ultimate achievements then your goal milestones are markers along the way to your dreams. Having your milestones in each area of your life mapped out in front of you is exciting, encouraging and motivating. Without milestone markers your ultimate goal seems so far away, too distant maybe, which may result in you not taking that journey at all. With milestone markers you can easily see the next challenge in front of you, which seems achievable, and ultimately leads to your dream goal.

Your life's milestones are essentially a mind map of your life which you use to set the goals that you want to achieve next. You can easily see what the next goal needs to be and you can see if you are moving in the right direction. Your life's milestones cover all aspects of your life including your personal life and your business.

Such areas of your life could be health, family, personal wealth, a particular business, travel, hobbies and interests, friends, assets and philanthropy. Other areas may come through to you from your intuition. These could be cars you want to drive, holiday properties you want to own, other businesses you would like to own or a career in the movies.

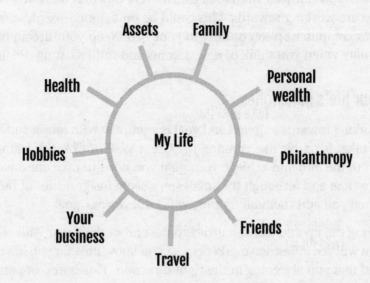

Within each of these areas of your life you will breakdown into milestones that you want to achieve. For example the milestones for travel could be places you want to visit or methods of travel you want to use. For hobbies it could be you want to have a fifteen handicap at golf or be able to play the piano.

You can then develop each of these milestones further. For the milestone *be able to play the piano* you may want to add sub-milestones of the things you want to achieve such as to be able to play your first song, be able to play a pop song by heart, be able to read music and to play in a concert.

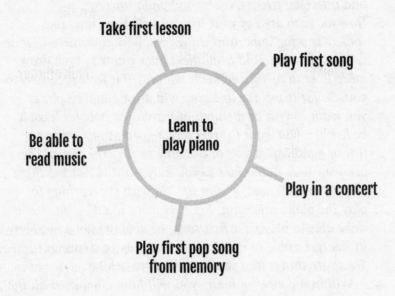

EXERCISE

3. *To get started on your life's milestones you will want a blank piece of paper, preferably A3, lots of different coloured pens and a few hours of distraction free time. You may even want to meditate before starting to relax and align yourself and possibly meditate throughout to be as connected as possible to your intuition.*

4. *Write 'My Life' in the middle of the paper and draw a circle around it. Next, while leaving space in between, write around this circle the areas of your life that are important to you, areas that already exist or areas that you want to exist. This is a spider diagram or mind map*

so you will circle around each area of your life and draw a line to your 'My Life' circle to link the areas with your inner circle.

Whatever comes to you as an area of your life you should write it down. If you get stuck use these to get started: health, family, personal wealth, a particular business, travel, hobbies and interests, friends, assets and philanthropy.

5. Now for each area of your life you will draw lines like spiders legs for important things you wish to achieve in that area of your life. And from these lines you may even draw more lines to further define it but only if it feels necessary to you. So for travel the lines you will draw could be places you want to visit or methods of travel. For hobbies it could be hobbies you want to start or get good at like having a fifteen handicap at golf or learning to play the piano. These are your life's milestones so you may want to develop them further in each area of your life. So with the learning to play the piano milestone you may want to add a milestone to be able to play your first song, be able to play a pop song by heart, be able to read music or to play in a concert. These are things that you would like to achieve.

Within a couple of hours you will have completed all the areas of your life and your milestones for each. Once completed take a step back and soak it in. This is your ideal life and working towards these milestones is your number one priority.

6. Looking at your life's milestones each day is motivating knowing that the next goal will lead you closer to your end goal and you will have focus for the day ahead on what you should be working on. It is also motivating to tick off the milestone markers as you complete them moving closer to the ultimate goal.

Rather than try to work on all areas of your life at once choose two or three milestones that you want to work towards now and focus your time and energy there. Make sure you are doing something daily to work towards those chosen milestones.

Reward yourself, with anything that you feel is appropriate, each time a milestone is met. And reward yourself with progress made towards each milestone as this helps to build momentum and it is momentum that makes it easier to achieve things.

When you tick off the milestones you have already met, choose from your chart another milestone to work towards so you are always working on two or three milestones at a time.

This is your life's work; it's not meant to be achieved in a year or two but over the course of your life. Working on your priorities will make sure you get the things that are most important to you done first and not leave you with any regrets when you look back at your life.

For some people, and the general consensus is that there is not one, single goal planning process that is right for everyone, this will be enough to help them create and achieve their goals because the milestones are effectively their goals. Having a rigid goal planning process can stifle some people but having a too open goal planning process can also lead to no progress.

The next part of this chapter is about creating goals with a particular process. Try the whole process to create your goals for a few months and then try the life's milestones as your goal planning process for a few months. See what gets you the best results and if neither are helpful to you then try something in between both methods. But if you get results from the first process and are happy with the process then stick with it, as you will continue to build momentum and make more opportunity for yourself.

Do please remember to focus on what you enjoy, love and what you do to bring value to others. And watch out for your ego getting in the way of wanting to do, have or be things for reasons that don't align with your authentic self, but are purely there to show off or be better than someone else. Ego goals are wasted time and energy.

Create a goal

There are two types of goals; personal goals and business goals. In some cases your personal goals will fuel your business goals because you will need time and money from your business to help you achieve your personal goals. Whether a goal is personal or business, it will follow the same process. With your chosen dream you are now going to add more structure to work towards it. You will fulfil your dream by turning it into a goal.

This may seem daunting at first but the process requires you to break the goal down into baby steps rather than a giant leap. That way you are taking manageable small steps towards your goal every day instead of doing nothing because the goal seems so big and hard to achieve.

All of your goals will follow the same formula when they are created. You will make them **SMART** goals.

Specific – You use lots of detail to describe what you want to achieve to make it feel as real as possible.

Measureable – You can easily track your progress to see how you are getting on compared to where you should be.

Achievable – Your goal isn't too easy but you feel that you can achieve it if you focus and work hard.

Relevant – Your goal is something that you definitely want to achieve, it is relevant to you, and it will make you feel awesome when you achieve it.

Timed – You have a deadline set for when your goal will be achieved and the timeframe is achievable. Nothing sharpens the focus of your mind like a deadline.

When you have a **SMART** goal it becomes clear in your mind what you are going to achieve and when you will achieve it.

An example of a non-**SMART** personal goal is: I want to run a marathon.

A **SMART** version of this personal goal could be: I want to run my first marathon in the New York marathon, next year, in under five hours. It's specific and progress can be measured through training. The average time for the New York Marathon is four and a half hours so under five hours is achievable but a stretch for a first time marathon, so it's relevant if you want to get into great shape and the deadline is the next year.

The key is to write your goals down. Once written down, the goal sinks into your subconscious mind and you start to work towards it. Writing it down makes it real.

Visualising yourself achieving your goals will help too. Think about how you will feel, what you will look like, what you will do and what you will hear when you achieve your goal. As you may know part of your brain thinks in pictures and it has no concept of time. So create a picture of your achievement through visualising it and your brain will think that it has achieved it already. This is very powerful to help you work towards your goals. And don't do this just once; do it weekly or monthly, every time you read your goals.

A study conducted by Dr Gail Matthews at Dominican University in California found people that had written goals accomplished much more – 50% more – than those who did not. The study also found that those people who had written goals and action commitments, sent them to a supportive friend and then sent weekly updates to their friend, accomplished significantly more – 78% more – than those who did not have written goals. So by writing down your goals, making commitments on your progress and having accountability from someone supportive means you are likely to accomplish 78% more than simply just thinking about your goals.

You may find it helpful to each year sit down with your spouse, partner or family and plan together what you want to achieve over the next twelve months. Use your dreams and their dreams to start the process for things you each want to be, do and have during the next year. And consider specific areas of your life such as your business, your career, your home, your holidays, your cars, your family, your lifestyle and your luxuries.

Once you have the list you can then write in present tense all the things you have done, achieved and become as if you have already achieved all of your goals – make sure to write how it made you feel. Including your emotions helps you to find motivation and helps to make the future seem even more possible. It's a bit like writing a diary entry one year from now looking back at what a great year it has been. By writing in this way it makes your subconscious believe that you have actually achieved those things and it's another way of putting it out there in the Universe for it to come back to you. Like visualisation, this is a really powerful step.

Next you can start to help make things happen by putting an estimated value of what is required to accomplish each item on the list. The total of the amounts is the amount of income you require over the next twelve months to accomplish everything on your list. In other words, this is the personal income you will need from your business, in addition to the cost of living if you haven't entered this on your list.

The next step is to prioritise the items so you both agree the order in which your accomplishments are made. Your top priorities will then become your personal goals for the year so write them down as **SMART** goals.

You can then create a **SMART** business goal to help fulfil that required income, which simply could be just to pay yourself more if there is enough profit and cash in the business.

My wife and I sit down each year to complete this activity. We really understand what the other person dreams about and what we want to achieve over the next twelve months to enable us to work out together how we will accomplish the things on our list. It is great fun too and really makes us focus on where we spend our time.

For example, if you knew that thirty-six new customers over the course of a year will give your business the required profit to pay yourself sufficient extra to accomplish one of your goals – say you want to get two weekend Paddock Passes at the Formula One Monaco Grand Prix – your **SMART** business goal may look like this: I want to obtain six leads per month to generate three new customers per month, using the existing conversion rate of 50%, every month for the next twelve months.

The focus every month will be getting six leads, maintaining the conversion rate of 50% and giving great service to those customers.

EXERCISE

*Write a **SMART** personal goal that immediately comes to mind. You may find it easier to simply write down something you want to achieve and then turn that in to a **SMART** goal:*

*Now write a **SMART** business goal, which may help you achieve your personal goal or it could simply be something you want to accomplish in your business.*

Pain and Gain

To make sure that you are motivated to achieve your goal the next step is write down the benefits you will receive and the losses to be avoided from achieving your goal.

Having a list of benefits and losses to be avoided helps you to focus on what is really motivating you to achieve your goal. You may find that the losses to be avoided are more powerful motivators than the benefits but most of the time you will find the benefit or positive outcome is a far more powerful motivator than the pain or negative outcome. This will be different for each goal but it is a key step for you to know why you want to achieve this goal. If **SMART** is a logical step then your motivation is an emotional step. Make sure your logic and emotion are in the same place to give the goal the best chance of being achieved.

The benefits and losses to be avoided will vary, depending on your goal and how you feel about them. Try to be as detailed as possible to really fire up the motivation. After the first attempt of writing them down, review the list and ask yourself 'do I feel motivated?' If not, then write more detail specific to you and the goal, get really personal with it. If after that list you still don't feel motivated or you struggle to write the benefits and losses to be avoided, then your goal isn't really a goal at all.

Do make sure that you connect with yourself on an emotional level to find the benefits and the pain otherwise what you write down will be superficial and they won't motivate you for long, if at all. A benefit such as 'it will make you feel good' or a pain such as 'it will cost you money' aren't emotional enough. You need to ask yourself how will it make you feel good and what does that mean to you. Having lots of energy when you wake up in the morning getting out of bed fired up ready to start your day is a pretty powerful motivator and that will make you feel good.

Carrying on the previous example a couple of benefits could be:

From the increased personal income you'll achieve a lifelong dream to attend the Formula One Monaco Grand Prix in style which may make you feel elated, ecstatic, complete, fulfilled, excited, confident,

25

strong and grateful. All of the emotions associated with an event you never want to end.

Your business will also have grown by thirty-six customers which may give you a sense of accomplishment, confidence to achieve more goals, make you proud that you have a real business and not a job, grateful to help those new customers, excited by the opportunity to help them further with your other services and products and happy you achieved what you set out to do.

A couple of losses to be avoided from achieving the goal could be:

Feeling stagnant and unmotivated by your inability to grow the business which could flow into your family life making you and your family miserable, sad and breakdown your relationship.

Watching the next Formula One Monaco Grand Prix on television instead of from hospitality at the Monte Carlo Casino will make you feel disappointed, sad, depressed, angry, hopeless and you may fall out of love altogether with the sport that you love so much.

The next step is to list all the possible obstacles that will prevent you from achieving your goal. Ask yourself the questions, what will stop me? Who will stop me? Why will this goal not be achieved?

Speak to someone you know who is either very critical or negative. You know the one – that person who tells you why something won't work and why your idea is a bad one. They are a gold mine for potential obstacles.

Now that you have the details of what will potentially stop you from achieving your goal you need to write a solution to each of these obstacles, line by line. Questions to ask yourself are: How can I stop this from happening? What can I do to turn this into a positive result?

Again, speak to your obstacle generator and ask them: Why? This will help you find the real problem, through their eyes, behind the obstacle so you can work on a solution for it.

You now have a detailed list of what you are going to achieve, why you are working towards it and how to tackle problems as they arise.

An obstacle will depend on your goal but it could be you and how you think that is an obstacle, having too much or too little of what is required to achieve the goal or how you spend your time.

Using the same example as before of obtaining six leads per month, a few possible obstacles could be:
- Too few quality leads
- Too many leads
- Poor conversion rate

So the solutions could be:
- Increase your marketing channels, rewrite the marketing copy to resonate more with your target market and use a different method of getting to your target market.
- Automate or delegate part of the sales process to a team member or virtual assistant so that you spend your time on the parts of the sales process that can only be done by you. Outsource, find capacity in your team or recruit to deal with the extra work. Make sure your process disqualifies the leads that don't tick all the boxes so you are left only with the leads that really want to work with you and you with them.
- Continue to monitor the conversion rate, implement new processes one at a time such as new scripts, information, additional communication touches with the prospective customer and measure the results for each change.

EXERCISE

Using your personal and business goals that you created on the previous exercise write down a couple of benefits and losses to be avoided by achieving each of those goals. Now write down a couple of obstacles and solutions for each of those goals.

Plan of Action

The next phase is to create action steps of what you need to do to achieve your goal. Just simply list everything that you need to do. It is best to think of this as baby steps towards your goals rather than giant leaps. So after getting your action steps written down, go through your list and see if you can break them down into smaller actions. The smaller the action the easier it will be to complete, which means, step by step, you are working towards your goal.

The more action steps you complete the more confidence and momentum you will create helping you achieve your goal by the deadline you set. Plus, if you are having a bad day or you look at the end goal and it seems too far away you know that you just need to do that one baby step today and that will get you closer.

Now you have written your list you need to number the action steps in order of what needs to be completed. Then write a target date next to each of your action steps. This is a good time to review the Timed element of your goal to see if it fits with your action steps. You may need to revise the end deadline to fit in all of the action steps.

Using the same example as before some of the action steps could be:
- Identify three marketing channels to use
- Identify your ideal customer profile
- Research your existing customers to find out what their problems are, how your business helps them and why they chose you
- Create a couple of lead magnets to give away
- Ensure marketing copy in each channel clearly includes your ideal customer profile
- Set up tracking and measurement processes for each channel
- Define the sales process once a lead is received
- Review your sales call script to ensure you disqualify out bad leads
- Review your sales brochure to make sure it is up to date to send to prospective customers
- Check your pricing and closing the sale process

Again there are two different schools of thought here. Very detailed plans with every baby step written down will work well for some people; having just the next two or three steps will work well for others. Find through trial and error what works best for you by measuring the progress and motivation you have over a specific amount of time for each process. And when you find your chosen plan of action process make sure you stick to it.

I had the opportunity to hear Sir Chris Hoy tell his story about how he became such an amazingly successful athlete. He talked about how it was his goal to become an Olympic gold medal winner when he first started cycling competitively. But rather than focus on the end goal of Olympic gold, he focused on the next step to get him there from where he was. Then when that step was complete he focused on the next step, then the next step and so on, which led ultimately to Olympic gold.

Sir Chris also followed the same process when his goal was to retain his gold medals. He would focus on the next thing he had to do on that day, then the next thing for the day after and so on. Even on a bad day when he was tired of the early morning training, he would just think about the next step, starting with getting out of bed and then eating breakfast, then getting showered, then getting dressed and so on, rather than think about the training that he momentarily didn't want to do. Those small steps were much more manageable and moved him closer to the goal for the day, which was to complete his training.

If you want to climb Mount Everest you have to do it one step at a time. Even though the thought of getting to the top is scary and seems like hard work you just focus on the next step that will get you that little bit closer to achieving your goal.

The final step of this phase is to understand how you are going to measure your goal. Again two schools of thought. Simply make sure you are moving in the right direction towards your milestones or add the key measurements of your goals to your weekly and monthly reporting to ensure you are on track. Identifying key milestones for your goals is a good idea so you know that when you hit them you are on track and you can reward yourself for the achievement so far. And if you don't hit your milestones on time you can check why and make revisions to your goals or how you spend your time.

Getting the right process for you will give you energy and feel easier.

EXERCISE

List the action steps required to achieve each of your personal and business goals that you had previously written and then number each action for each goal in order of priority.

Take action

Making sure you take action is next and by this point you will be champing at the bit to get on with it because you have a well thought out and planned goal that is now somehow really achievable.

Before taking action though let someone else have a copy of your goal planning. They will then be able to hold you accountable to your action plan and help you if you get stuck. It's best to find someone supportive outside of your business who is objective and will ask you the right and sometimes hard questions.

If you have a bad day or find the overall task daunting just remember Sir Chris Hoy and his quest for a gold medal at the Olympics. If that still doesn't help then revisit your goal planning and try to add more pain and gain and more action steps. And if that still doesn't motivate you then perhaps the goal isn't really a goal for you, or it can be parked for a later date because it is not a priority now.

Each day you will want to work on the things that are most important to you and the things that only you can do. Working towards your goals is one of these things, so schedule time each day to work on the action steps and read your goals.

You may want to work on this first, before other tasks like reading emails, making calls or completing technical work, so that if your day doesn't go as planned then you know that at least you completed your action step for the day and you are still working towards your goals.

Then at the end of each day review what you have worked on to make sure you have done the right things with your time and the action step for the day was completed. After, plan the next day, schedule an appointment with yourself to work on the next action step.

Also schedule time each month to plan your goals for the month ahead and review your current goals to make sure they are still relevant and that you are on track.

When you have more than one goal you need to prioritise the action steps you will work on. This will be based on how important each goal is to you and how much time you are prepared to put aside to work towards these goals. You may be able to run two or three goals at the same time quite easily, but more than this and you may find it difficult to keep up and are likely to lose momentum and confidence, which may lead to you giving up on that goal. Make sure that you do not give yourself too much to do. Well planned goals are the key to scheduling the time required to work towards your goals.

Don't forget to acknowledge your progress for each baby step and each big step towards your goal with a reward. It can be anything that you will enjoy, like going for a walk, playing Xbox, going to the cinema or buying a new guitar.

Get a complete goal planning template for personal and business goals at www.stevenbriginshaw.com/profitsbonus.

EXERCISE

Write down a list of things you like or want to do. These can be things you do every day or things you don't do enough of, such as: going for a walk, sitting in the garden, listening to music, playing music on your favourite instrument, buying yourself a treat, spending time with someone you admire, making a trip, going on holiday, buying some new shoes or watching a movie.

Use this list for your rewards for your actions and completion of your goals.

If you completed all of the exercises in this chapter you will now have a personal and a business goal fully written and planned with a list of rewards for yourself for each step you make towards achievement.

Real world thoughts

I am very fortunate because dreaming comes naturally to me. I'm a dreamer and I love dreaming about wonderful possibilities and how they make me feel. My dreams are mostly about experiences, a little about possessions and some about the legacy I am working towards.

I want to share my big dream with you. My dream of the future that I will have a role in fulfilling. By the way, this clarity didn't come to me overnight; it took patience, self-exploration and listening to myself to get to this point, which may change in the future.

I dream of a time where entrepreneurs all over the world run their own extraordinary business in their favourite niche, delighting their customers, fulfilling their own dreams and making their own mark on the Universe. All entrepreneurs spreading happiness and gratitude through the world by doing what they love.

I dream about entrepreneurship and business being taught in primary and secondary schools so children at the age of sixteen and above can make a more informed decision about their future. Starting and running a business will be a serious option that is available in addition to getting a job, enrolling in more education to help with a future career, or choosing something to study, to buy more time to decide what to do next.

I dream of creating an entrepreneur university where school leavers and adults of all ages can enrol on the only program the university teaches; how to start and run an extraordinary business built around what they love to do. With tutors from the world of business educating and supporting the students to learn and experience the business world, with all its downs and ups, in a safe environment. Where ideas and dreams can be fine-tuned or changed as necessary to find the right puzzle pieces for each student. The end result being graduation with the knowledge, experience and support that will give each entrepreneur the life and business they dream about while making the world a slightly better place.

Every time I share or think about this it feels me with happiness, motivation, wonderment and a sense of inevitability. With patience and practice you will feel the same way too, if you don't already.

Here's a more personal dream I have:

I dream about seeing the Earth from Space where I will marvel in awe of the beauty of our planet and be in a state of appreciation and wonderment at how miraculous we are as beings on Earth, how our planet came to exist and how tiny our planet and we are compared to the rest of our Solar System, our Galaxy and the Universe.

Taking time to think about this always amazes me and fills me with gratitude.

If dreaming doesn't come that easy to you then schedule sixty minutes or so to relax and do nothing. Sit in the garden or in your favourite chair and listen to your thoughts, don't do anything with them, just listen. When you feel at ease and comfortable ask yourself, 'What do I dream about?' and listen to what comes back. Write it down or speak it into a voice recorder. The more you do it the more in tune you will get with your dreams. When you feel more at ease follow the dream map process and the life's milestone process.

Planning and goal setting are processes to follow and finding the right process for you is the key so experiment. Try one way and then try another to see what works best for you.

I do find goal planning a little tricky sometimes particularly linking the emotional pain and gain side to my plans. I've learned that when I can't link enough emotion and feeling to a goal it means I don't really want it, possibly ever, but certainly not now.

I experiment a lot with goal planning and, contrary to the **SMART** method of goal planning, I am currently testing whether dropping the T, the timed element of **SMART**, is helpful to me in understanding more about myself, or whether it helps me achieve the goals I have struggled with because I have previously felt too much pressure to achieve it.

My least strong point in the process is rewarding myself for progress. I have to really concentrate and schedule in rewards. I too have a list of my rewards for little steps and big steps towards my dreams to make it easier for me to think of a reward and actually reward myself. In the past the rewarding part of the process did seem less significant to me but it is a key part of building momentum to achieve what you want in life and it's cool.

Make sure you reward yourself too for your little and big steps.

CHAPTER SUMMARY

Key points

- Dream again like you did when you were a child and dream big.
- Get your dreams out of your head either on to a vision map, sound map or mood map depending on your preferred learning/communication style. Revisit your map regularly to visualise your dreams.
- Having written goals with written action commitments and regularly sending them to a supportive person to hold you accountable will help you achieve 78% more.
- Start with baby steps, they're easier to manage, and lead towards giant leaps.
- Schedule time to work on your goals before you work on anything else.
- Reward yourself for progress, even the smallest amount of progress, it will help build momentum.

Exercise checklist

Tune into your dreams

Write down a couple of dreams in each of what you want to be, do and have

Create your dreams map (either a vision map, sound map or mood map)

Create your life's milestones

*Write a **SMART** personal goal and a **SMART** business goal*

Write down the benefits, losses to be avoided, the obstacles and solutions for your personal and business goals

List the action steps for your goals and then number in order of priority

Create your rewards list

Get a personal and business goal planning template at www.stevenbriginshaw.com/profitsbonus

KNOW WHAT YOUR BUSINESS NEEDS TO DO
Link your goals to the numbers

Most of your goals will require some money for you to achieve them so it is important to know how you will get your hands on the cash you need.

The easiest way is for your business to generate this cash. After all, your business is the vehicle to achieve your dreams. So what does the business need to do to get the required amount of cash?

To find out, create a budget for the business for the year in which you feel the business will be finished. 'Finished' means when you feel you have accomplished all you want with the business, your endgame. This may be in five years, ten years or 100 years. But that is the starting point. You are starting with the end in mind. Make sure that you include enough profit after tax to be able to afford your goals.

The budget for the year of your endgame will need to show your sales, direct costs and fixed costs to calculate your profit. Also estimate the business tax that will be due and calculate your profit after tax. But you should also know in great detail the other key numbers, with your goals in mind, such as:
- Number of customers
- Average sale amount per customer
- Average number of purchases per customer
- Who your ideal customer is
- What you sell
- The business valuation
- The size of your team
- Your locations of work
- Your take home pay
- The hours you work per week etc

Some of this will be guess work but it will help you understand what you are working towards. But you will have a good idea of what you want your business to be like when it is finished. And it is really exciting seeing your dream business appear before you.

By the way, just in case you need an explanation, direct costs are those costs that relate directly to generating sales, which you will only incur if you make a sale. Fixed costs are those costs that you have to pay regardless of whether you make any sales or not.

EXERCISE

To help you get started, fill in the numbers and answer the questions below. Complete the 'Now' column first and enter the figures for each line based on what these numbers are right now. Then enter your ideal numbers in the 'Future' column. Write a number above the future column to confirm how many years away the future column is.

	Now	Future
Turnover		
Net profit		
Number of customers		
Team members numbers		
Locations where you sell		
Take home pay per month		
Hours worked per week		

Who are the customers? What do you provide to your customers?

Who are your team? How big a team do you have? What role do you play in your business at your endgame? Is your business virtual or do you have premises? Where are the premises?

Next, you can work backwards each year until you get to today. Completing the same tasks and entering the same figures as you did for your endgame year. So if your endgame year is in five years' time you will also have a column for years four, three, two, and one, along with a column for where your business is right now.

What you will have done is created the road map of your business goals broken down by year. You will actually enjoy doing this because it somehow makes your dreams feel real by linking them to your numbers.

Planning more than a year into the future may be uncomfortable or scary to you but stick with it as you will find it liberating to have such clarity for the next few years. It makes life simpler because the decisions you make will be linked to your plans. If something doesn't get you towards your plan then you won't do it, if it does you will. It reduces the amount of grey area to almost become totally black and white.

Do be aware that you will likely over estimate what you can achieve in the short term and under estimate what you can achieve in the long term. Also be aware that things may not go to plan. Your business purpose may change, your goals and dreams may change or you may achieve your goals in a shorter time. The plan is simply a plan, something to work towards but needs to be flexible with changing opportunities and challenges that come your way.

You now have a year by year overview of what you expect your business to look like.

EXERCISE

- *Look at your forecast for year one and compare that to now. Here are some questions to help.*
- *What are the differences? Are they realistic?*
- *How many more customers do you need? How many is that per month?*
- *How many more team members do you need to make it a reality? When do you need them?*
- *What do you need to do differently to get the results for*

Year one? Do you need to change the way you think about yourself and your business?
- *How are you going to measure these numbers each month?*

Now you will need to get a bit more detailed by creating a budget for the next twenty-four months, which will agree with your Year one and Year two overview figures, detailing month by month how much your sales, direct costs and fixed costs will be. You will get the most out of this if you do it line by line for each sale, direct and fixed cost. Use your previous year's income and expenditure as a guide.

You now have a month by month target to hit for the next twenty-four months, which you know is part of your overall goal for the business. Each month you can check the actual performance of the business against your budget and can create an action plan to maintain or improve the performance of the business.

You will see very clearly if the numbers can support your goals over the next twenty-four months and if the numbers are realistic.

You should also create a cash flow forecast for the next twenty-four months as this will show you and your bank manager if you need any funding in the future to help with your business growth.

A cash flow forecast is in principle the same as a budget but looks at the cash movement date rather than sales or cost incurred date. The reason for this is that you will pay some of your suppliers on credit terms, say thirty days, and you may offer your creditworthy customers some form of credit terms too. This means that a cost incurred this month will not be due for payment until the next month. The cash flow forecast will show this timing difference.

Taking a cash flow forecast and budget to your bank manager months in advance of any problems will allow the bank enough time to make a better, more informed decision. Especially if your cash flow forecast shows a return to having cash in the bank in the months after the cash requirement.

You will also be able to compare the monthly actual cash movement in your business to the forecast and see if you are on track or not and then take action to improve or maintain things in the next month.

EXERCISE

Complete your yearly endgame plan and your month by month twenty-four month budget and cash flow forecast. This will involve guess work so use your best guess for now to get a stick in the sand, it can always be updated later.

Get simple templates to start on your yearly plan and month by month twenty-four month budget and cash flow forecast at www.stevenbriginshaw.com/profitsbonus.

Your personal goals and your twenty-four month budget will provide the information to create your business goals. You will see clearly what you have to achieve from the budget so all you need to do is follow the goal process from the previous chapter for your business goal; write the **SMART** business goal down, write down the pain and gain, obstacles and solutions and then the step by step action plan with deadlines – and get accountability from someone external to your business.

It's a great idea to involve your team or your family as they will be able to help you brainstorm ideas, for action steps to help achieve the goals. They will also know where you want to be, what you are doing and why you want to get there and they will feel part of the process. It's good fun too so they and you will enjoy it.

Your business organisation chart

To achieve your business goals you will need to know what your business will look like from a team point of view and who will be doing what in the business to make things happen. This applies even if currently there is just you in your business.

The same principle applies here, you want to draw the organisation chart with all of the team member roles at the point when your business is finished, when you've reached your endgame. Then you will want to create an exact copy of the endgame chart and write next to each position who is currently fulfilling that role. It's not uncommon to have one name in more than one role.

By having a visual plan of how your team will look and who is responsible for other team members it gives you a clear picture of what you need to achieve from now to your endgame. It also helps with planning who to hire first and when you will step out of multiple roles.

In a typical organisation chart there will be a Chief Executive Officer (CEO) who sits above the director for each of marketing, sales, operations and finance. Under each director will be managers and each manager will be responsible for the remaining team members. In most small businesses however the managers section isn't required and the directors will effectively be the managers looking after their respective team. Administrative and IT support may also be required for each area of the business and they tend to report to the operations director.

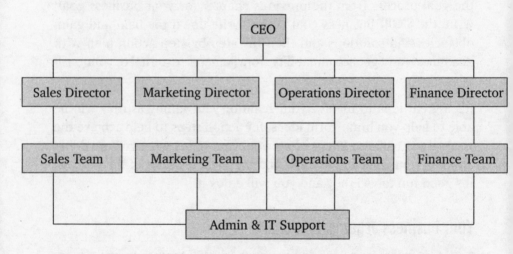

The CEO will focus on strategy, culture, innovation and product/service development for the whole business. The directors report to the CEO who will hold them accountable for their respective areas of the business.

The directors will focus on strategy and planning, be responsible for managing, hiring, firing and training their respective team, reviewing and approving systems improvements and they may complete high level work that their team cannot complete.

The team members in each area will complete the day to day work of the business.

Not all roles in the business have to be full time, particularly as your business is growing. You may only need a part time finance director or a part time marketing director. And not all of the roles need to be employees. They can be outsourced to self employed job owners or other businesses. For example you could have a marketing consultant to act as your marketing director and marketing team. You could have an outsourced bookkeeper to act as your finance team and a virtual finance director. The most common part time or outsourced role is admin support.

Within your business you will want every role in your team, including yours, to have accountability to someone else and to your business goals. The best way to do this is to have key performance indicators (KPIs) for each role that are linked to your business goals and are within the control of each role. This measures the performance of each and every team member in your business and the progress towards your endgame. Targets will be set for each role, in line with your business goals, and these will be compared to the actual performance each month. From there it is a simple question of was the target met or not and asking the team member why the results are as they are, good or bad. Then the team members can suggest ways to improve or maintain their performance.

For example, you will most likely want to measure your marketing team on the number of leads received, the number of those leads that fit your ideal client profile, the cost per lead and more detailed analysis of each marketing method used. You will measure the important factors in each area of your business that will lead to your business success.

For each role in your business you will need to write down the duties and KPIs, even if you are currently fulfilling those roles. This gives a clear understanding of what is required of each role and how they will be measured. It will also help with recruitment as you will have a good outline of a job description.

You can download a list of the typical roles within a business and what they do from www.stevenbriginshaw.com/profitsbonus.

EXERCISE

- *If you used the example organisation chart on the previous page as the organisation chart for your business or drew your own, which role would you have when you have reached your endgame? Remember, you don't have to be the CEO even though it is your business.*
- *Now look at the example organisation chart again, which roles are you currently completing?*
- *Which roles are you able to relinquish first and why those roles?*
- *By understanding your answers to these questions you will have a clearer picture of what your business will look like, how it will work and you can add the recruitment of team members to your plans.*

Your role in the business

Now you have worked out your goals and how they fit within your business you now need to understand what your role will be within the business.

Your business can be divided up into two areas. Strategy and Operation.

Strategy means focusing on the long term view of the business by working on the business model, goal planning, leading, innovating, motivating, systemising, training and educating. This is working ON your business.

Operation means focusing on the day to day view of the business by working on the technical work, sales, administration, finance, marketing, operations and customer experience. Working IN your business.

To start with you will work in both areas of your business but as your business grows you will need to spend more time in the strategy area. As the business owner you should do the things that only you can do. Everything else can be delegated or outsourced for someone else to do. This is because your time is extremely valuable and you need to spend it doing the things that will give you the biggest return.

Having a clear goal will provide clarity of your journey so you will know exactly what needs to be done to achieve your dreams. Being a great leader will help you inspire and motivate your team to pull in the same direction and achieve your dreams much quicker and their dreams too.

Doing the bookkeeping in your business or answering the phone will not help you get to where you are going, so these operational tasks can be performed by someone else.

It is possible that you like doing some of the operational tasks so the ideal situation is to be in a position where you can choose what you do with your time. Having a CEO to focus on strategy and systemisation so you can do the selling is one possibility.

From linking your goals to the numbers in your business you will know how much time you want to spend working on and in the business. So what else are you going to do with your time?

Your personal goals may give you an idea of what you will be doing. Perhaps you will go on more holidays with your family or spend time perfecting your hobbies.

The key is to know what you enjoy and what you are passionate about and this will help you understand what you will do with your time. This may not be possible now because of a lack of time or money or you simply don't know yet but this is what you are working towards.

EXERCISE

Over the next week write down all of the tasks you have completed and how much time in hours you have spent on each task. Then mark each task you have completed as either 'ON' for working on your business or 'IN' for working in your business. Add up the total hours for IN, the total hours for ON and the total hours worked that week. Ideally it is best to keep a note of your task and time as you progress through the day.

Tasks	Hours Spent
Total hours spent IN your business	
Total hours spent ON your business	
Grand total of hours	

Here's a link to get a more detailed template time tracker from www.stevenbriginshaw.com/profitsbonus.

I remember when I kept timesheets as a junior trainee accountant and I would write up my time at the end of the day. The trouble was at the end of the day I couldn't remember everything I had done. I would always end up with an hour or three unaccounted for. I quickly learned to keep track of my tasks and my time. If you've ever kept timesheets you may have experienced the same thing. So definitely keep a note of your time as you go through the day.

To be honest I really dislike timesheets but for this purpose they are insightful.

From the results you'll be able to see where you are spending your time and you will also see the percentage of your time that you are spending IN and ON your business (divide your IN time by the total time and your ON time by the total time). If your IN time percentage is higher than your ON time percentage or higher than you expected then you need to seriously consider what IN tasks you can either delegate, outsource or eliminate from your week so that you can spend more time working ON your business.

After identifying the tasks you want to delegate or outsource you will want to make sure the person taking over those tasks can get the same consistent results as you.

What do you want to do with the business when it is finished

In my experience you will want to do one of three things with your business when it is finished. Sell it, pass it on to family or to have a role in your business for as long as you live, doing what you love.

In order to achieve any of the three outcomes or endgames you will need to do the same, one thing. Systemise your business.

If you have a fully systemised business it will have a massively higher value, so you can sell it for more money. As a general rule of thumb a generic non systemised business will sell for a multiple of one to five of the net profit. A generic systemised business will sell for a multiple of five to ten of the net profit. So you could increase the value of your business by as much as ten times by fully systemising it. Some valuation methods are more specific to a niche or sector like financial services and professional services where a multiple of turnover is often used. The point is the same though; the more systemised your business, the more it will be worth.

If you have a fully systemised business it will be easy for your loved ones to run and continue to make money from the hard work you put in to the business. Or it will make it much easier and more valuable for your family if they decide to sell it.

If you have a fully systemised business it will allow you to spend your time as you see fit and earn from the business until you pass away because your team will be able to follow the systems to get the same great results each and every time. And once you pass away your family or your team will be able to continue to get the same great results or to easily and more valuably sell the business.

Have an idea of which one of the three you want to work towards but having a systemised business allows you to change your mind as many times as you like or take opportunities that come your way.

Part of your dream may be to franchise or licence your business to other business owners so having a systemised business will be key so the other business owners can follow your processes exactly and get the same results.

Your systems will be the 'how to' manual to complete each task and role in your business.

It's a good idea to get a valuation of your business each year so you can plan appropriately for tax but also ensure that you are working towards the value that you desire.

But be aware that whichever of the endgames you are working towards, it will take time to prepare. It will take somewhere between twelve to thirty-six months to prepare for a sale and six to eighteen months to fully systemise your business depending on what you do, what systems you have now and how much time you are prepared to work on this. Using a professional to help you systemise your business will speed things up but it will be a big investment so make sure you have the spare cash and time to get them in.

There is a more detailed chapter on systemisation at the end of the book but resist the urge to jump to this chapter as the chapters in between will become part of your systems.

Your team involvement

Getting your team to buy in to your vision of the business is really important. They will need to know why you are doing what you are and how they fit in. If you don't have a team at the moment this is still important for you to know as you will have a team soon.

Asking your team to help with the goal planning is one way to involve them but you also need to make sure the team are doing the right things to work towards your goals. So it is sensible to ask them to review what they have done each day to make sure they are doing their bit to work towards achieving the goals. You could ask certain team members to plan their time like you do but this may not be workable or necessary for all team members.

Meeting regularly with your team is a good idea to report on the progress of the action plan and it will give you an opportunity to discuss what needs to be done over the next month to keep to the required action steps. It is also helpful to understand current issues, opportunities, customer complaints, customer feedback, innovation etc. Your team are the eyes and ears of your business so you will want the facts from them and their ideas, but don't have a meeting for the sake of it and don't keep the team longer than is necessary as they have important work to do. Also don't have a meeting to generate ideas, you will get more valuable input from your team if you ask them to brainstorm on their own and each of them report their own ideas at a meeting.

You could also get your team to help you systemise the business by creating a manual for their role but they will need to know why as they may feel that you are trying to replace them.

This will also lead naturally to asking your team for their personal goals. By knowing what they want to be, do and have you will be able to tie your business goals to their personal goals. Incentivising and rewarding your team based on helping them achieve their goals, because they are helping to achieve your goals, is a great win/win situation. Instead of a cash bonus you can pay for tickets to their favourite musician's concert or you can agree to Friday afternoons off so they can spend time with their family. These are just a couple of examples of what their dreams may be and how you can help your team achieve their goals through helping you achieve yours. Rewarding the team with help towards their goals is fantastic motivation and creates a common objective to succeed. This is far more rewarding and personal than a cash bonus.

Before you can reward your team members you will need to measure how they are doing. Common measures such as hours spent working or the number of outputs made, such as new customers gained or pieces of work sent out, will most likely be a poor measure. These miss the point of measuring success. But if you are in the business of only gaining new customers and not servicing them and keeping them then the example measurement is just fine.

The measurement of team performance must be aligned with your business goals and must be in the control of the team member. Otherwise it will be pointless.

So what do your team do and how does it link to your business goals?

Start with your business goals so you have a clear idea of what your team should be doing and then drill down into how they can make this happen within their role. Set them a monthly target for each measurement and then review the results each month, getting the teams feedback on what can be done to either maintain the results or improve them.

When targets are met within the agreed deadline or exceeded then that is the time to reward your team members by helping them with their goals.

I know a business owner that has just three measures for each of their client managers. The customer feedback score for the month, the number of extra work they bill in the month and how happy they feel.

The business owner knows that if the targets are hit for each of these measures then the business is working toward his business goals. Each measurement is within the teams control because they have everything they need through systemisation and training to be successful in these areas. Plus the team know they are also working towards their personal goals and already buy in to why the business does what it does.

Help your team create their goals by using the goal process in the previous chapter and ask them to report back to you so that you can help them achieve their goals.

Real world thoughts

Being a numbers and strategy person, I love this chapter. I find it really fun to work out the business model (strategy) starting with my required level of profit or knowing what I want my take home pay to be. Seeing the business come to life in my imagination is exciting and inspiring. This is where dreaming helps again as you will be dreaming into the future about the life and business you want.

By putting those dreams, no matter how wild, down on to paper with a business model and some numbers makes it feel very real. Like it is just a matter of time before this can help, providing there are not holes in the business model.

If you're not a numbers person or find it hard to see how business works then this bit can still be fun and enable you to see the bigger picture of your business but you may need to work with someone else to help you get more clarity.

All of the roles in the organisation chart of my first few businesses were always me to start with, I did everything. When I grew the business a little I would then bring someone else in to help with admin in the first instance and then someone else for operations. I enjoy selling, marketing and finance so I kept those roles as well as being the CEO and being the operations director.

It sounds a lot right? It was and for three of those roles I didn't do them justice because I simply had split up my focus and energy in to too many things.

Starting on your own and adding people as you grow the business is one way to get towards your dreams but this is slow, hard and can leave you needing a two week holiday every three months.

Through learning from other people and experimenting I have found an easier and quicker way. Before I even sold anything in my most recent business it started with a team and the business was profitable from day one. This was accomplished by getting the customers on board with an agreed start date and then getting the team in place to start from day one. The team are paid on a per job basis rather than a flat rate so if there are no sales then there are no team payments. Everyone works from home so there are no costs for things like rent or rates.

At the beginning I worked closely with them to systemise the areas of the business they looked after and now they run like a well-oiled machine with very little input from me. We continue to have team meetings and I help resolve queries every now and again but it leaves me to focus on what I want to do in the business rather than having to do it all.

Team in place, check. Profitable, check. That has saved me countless hours and stress compared to doing it the way I had with my previous businesses.

That business has a team of three at time of writing and we're getting it fully systemised before we start to grow it.

My role in each business has changed somewhat as I've progressed through my entrepreneurial journey. At the moment my role is to learn more about myself, others and business in general. Create content, new products and services based on my experiences and use this to help me educate, mentor and coach other entrepreneurs on their business journey.

I will still lead the team, plan ahead, review the business strategy, have some part in operations and drop into sales every now and again. Ultimately though it is my responsibility to have fun and do the things I enjoy, making sure I have space outside of business.

I've always intended to keep my businesses for the long term but things change. Looking back now I had no choice but to sell my accountancy practice because it was making me miserable and I didn't enjoy the work anymore. The clients were great and it was them that kept me involved with it, but I realised I had to put myself first and then make sure my clients got a good home. Your plans today for the future of the business may not be the same plans as tomorrow and that's fine because we all change. If you follow the **PROFITS** Principles in this book you'll be prepared for those changes.

CHAPTER SUMMARY

Key points

- Link your goals to the numbers in the business so your business can give you the cash you need for your goals and start at the point in the future when you've achieved your endgame.
- Start at your endgame in the future and work back year by year to one year from now.
- A 24 month budget and cash flow forecast will help you see any potential obstacles in your plans and you can use them to check the actual performance of your business is on track.
- Having an organisation chart of your endgame business will help you see the important roles required in your business, help you decide which roles to fill first and help you identify your ideal role in your business so you can work towards fulfilling only this role.
- Get buy in from your team by sharing your vision and plans and help them achieve their goals by linking them to your business goals.

Exercise checklist

Write down where you are now and where you want to be

Compare your forecast for year one to where you are now

Create an endgame yearly plan and a month by month budget and cash flow forecast for the next twenty-four months

Create your endgame organisation chart and questions on your role and hiring your next team member

Review your time spent working IN versus working ON your business

Get your yearly planner template, twenty-four month budget and cash flow forecast template, detailed roles in a business and time tracker at www.stevenbriginshaw.com/profitsbonus

YOUR MINDSET
Your authentic self

Doing things that you don't enjoy or that you aren't very good at (and don't plan to be) is horrible and hard work. It takes up more of your time to complete, more of your energy, even just thinking about doing it, and it requires more effort from you to get done to an acceptable standard.

Doing things you love or are naturally good at and have an interest in is amazing and fun. It feels like it is effortless, it gives you more energy and time seems to stand still. That's because you are in your flow, you are being your authentic self.

Every time you are the person you are supposed to be you experience the amazing and fun side of life. Every time you are trying to be someone or something else you experience the horrible and hard work side of life.

How would it make you feel if your life was amazing and fun every day? I would guess you would feel pretty complete, happy, loved, abundant, motivated and grateful. That's what will happen if you are your authentic self.

Authentic self just means being who you naturally are, just being yourself. Sure you will have a positive and negative side of yourself like everyone does but that's what makes you who you are, that's your authenticity. There is yin and yang to everything in life and that makes up the whole. A great example of this is in Star Wars. There is the dark side (the Empire, the Sith or the First Order) and the light side (the Jedi).

It sounds easy and straight forward, because it is, but it can be a difficult task to find your authentic self. You need to first accept yourself for who you are, the positive and the negative. Acknowledge the negative side of you and the negative emotions you feel, don't let the positive side of you think that the negative side doesn't exist. By acknowledging the negative or dark side of yourself you will become more self-aware and more awareness leads you to becoming more authentic.

Once aware of your negative feelings and thoughts you can then explore what that part of you means by asking yourself questions such as, 'what does this feeling mean to me'? Or 'where does the feeling come from'? Or 'what is this feeling trying to help me achieve'? Never ask yourself why you feel a particular way as your ego will answer the question and not your true self.

After a period of time you will accept yourself for who you really are and not see a positive or negative side. You will just see yourself as who you are, your authentic self. You will simply be yourself.

It is a continuing process and you will need to work on this regularly, it's like peeling back the layers of an onion and it keeps going and going. It may seem like a lot of effort but feeling amazing and having fun every day is certainly worth the effort instead of feeling horrible and life being hard work.

You are here for a reason and in my opinion it would be a travesty to not fulfil your potential and contribute your true self to the world.

When you are more in tune with yourself you can start to explore and express yourself more to help discover what you naturally love, what you are good at and how you can help others. You can discover this by writing in a journal to yourself, writing a blog to share with others, meditating to align and connect with yourself, recording your thoughts on a voice recorder or on video. The more you do it the easier it gets and the more realisations and more value you will find.

After you discover what you are good at and what you enjoy you should do more of these things and less of everything else. As a result you will stay in your flow and be the person you are meant to be. This will lead to you going big on the things that you love and enjoy in each area of your life (your hobbies, your health, yourself, your work, your family and friends, etc) and you will be able to let go of the other distractions.

I decided to do this with my life and started with my hobbies or the things I wanted to actively pursue to get good at. I wrote a list of all the things I enjoy doing (playing golf, playing guitar, playing Xbox, astronomy, reading, watching football, watching Formula One, weight training, learning about performance cars, listening to music and going to the cinema weekly) and chose one that I will dedicate myself to doing. One where I will focus my energy and effort for myself and for no one else, one I will go big on.

Once I had the list in front of me it was an easy decision that I will go big on guitar playing. I love playing the guitar and have been playing since I was eight years old, although I stopped playing when I was fourteen to instead mess around with my friends and chase girls. I love learning to play new songs and I love messing around playing my own chords and notes to hear what sounds good. It satisfies both sides of my brain, my right (creative, play) and left brain (logical, patterns, progress), and I simply love making and listening to the music.

I didn't drop everything else completely though. As a treat for progress towards my goals I will play Xbox or look up at the stars and planets or go to a football match or go to the cinema. These things along with listening to music also give me play time when I can relax and have fun for the sake of having fun. That's all they are to me now, treats and play time, rather than a serious hobby I am doing regularly and trying to get good at.

I didn't drop reading, I read non-fiction books mostly on business, self-awareness and the occasional autobiography, because I saw this as part of my authentic self to learn in order to create and have fun. I didn't drop weight training either, but took it as a fun activity rather than a means to an end, as I saw this as a basic need to look after my health, thus enabling me to have fun, learn, create and educate. Things that I see as essential to being who I am.

This inspired me to then look at all the other areas of my life and write down what was important to me or what each area meant to me. I could see a pattern emerging as I wrote, so I counted the number of times I used particular words to describe what each area of my life meant to me.

The words most repeated were fun/happiness, thinking/learning/meditating, creating and educating. I could then see that thinking/learning/meditating were fun and made me happy, this also enabled me to create, which is also fun and makes me happy. Thinking/learning/meditating and creating allow me to educate myself and others, which also leads to fun and happiness. This blew my mind!

Accidentally I had worked out who I am and why I am here on Earth; the things that really float my boat. To have fun, learn, create, educate and inspire that in others.

I then saw that this fitted perfectly with my love of business, numbers and entrepreneurship. This led me to understand that my reason for being here is me having fun and learning about myself, others and business to create products, services and tools from my own experiences, to educate and support entrepreneurs all over the world on their business journey. Enabling them to create and run an extraordinary business doing what they love, helping people they enjoy being with, and living the life they've dreamed of.

With that realisation my energy, motivation, happiness, determination instantly and dramatically went through the roof! I couldn't wait to get focused on my ideal life, part of which is sharing this book with you. Thank you for helping me do that.

EXERCISE

- *Write below a list of all of the hobbies that you have currently and have had in the past. Once you have the list in front of you ask yourself, 'If I had a magic wand and I could spend unlimited time, energy and money on just one hobby, a hobby I will go big on, which hobby will I choose?'*
- *When you have chosen that hobby commit to going big on it and letting go of your other hobbies.*
- *If you feel inspired after this exercise, as I did, create on a separate piece of paper a spider diagram of the areas of your life and ask yourself 'What does this area of my life mean to me?' and 'What is important to me in this area of my life?'.*

Why did you start your business?

When you started your business it was for a reason. Maybe to be your own boss, get the money you deserve or to better help your ideal customers. Your decision was made because you felt you could do something or be something to make a difference.

Having clarity of your 'Why' will help you to better understand how and what you do.

You may have lost your why because it is easy to get caught up in the day to day of running a business and not yet fulfilling what you set out to do.

Being a business owner is hard work because you are responsible for everything in the business and you must keep and win new customers, report and keep an eye on the finances, deal with the administration, manage and lead your team, look to innovate and improve existing services, focus on the existing and future strategy of the business, train and improve yourself as well as the team and market the business to your ideal customer. Much more than just delivering what you are good at or sticking to your why.

Or you may simply not have enough time for your why because you are so busy doing other stuff.

EXERCISE

- *Ask yourself, what was your reason for starting the business?*
- *Why does your business do what it does?*
- *Are you achieving what you set out to do?*

If you are like 80% of business owners out there, you are working at least 50-hour weeks and taking home much less than the national minimum wage because of the long hours that you work and because there isn't enough money to pay yourself what you would really like to receive.

So how do you move into the other 20%? You need to rediscover your Why.

You are you for a reason and you are here for a reason. You have the skills, knowledge, passion, beliefs and values for a reason. You just need to fit these together and bring this into your business to really achieve what you want.

You have your skills and expertise to help certain people. Your beliefs and values are the reason you do certain things and make certain decisions.

When you understand what you are passionate about it gives you clarity of purpose. You understand why you do the things you do and what you are working towards. Your passion will get you out of bed in the morning. And the things you enjoy will be linked to your passion.

You may feel that you do not know what your passion is or understand enough detail about it. That's fine because you can now start discovering it.

EXERCISE

Here are some questions to help you become more aware of yourself to give you more clarity.
- *What would be missing in the world if you were not here?*
- *If you already had all the money you would ever need, what would you do with your time?*
- *What are you good at?*
- *What do you enjoy doing?*
- *What do you believe in?*
- *What is your passion?*
- *What are your values?*
- *What do you get paid for?*

You can also ask your close friends and family the same questions about you as they will give you an answer that you may not even think about. And ask your customers why they work with you.

Why your 'Why' is important

You may feel this is a bit fluffy and has nothing to do with business. You will be right and wrong.

Yes it is fluffy, in that it is an area in which you may not be comfortable or have much experience. So it will be hard and you will have to fight yourself to work on it.

And it has everything to do with business.

Once you know what your why is, you will attract other people that are the same as you. Your ideal customers, ideal team members, ideal suppliers, ideal partners etc. They will want to work with you because they have the same passion, beliefs and values as you and know you will be able to help them. You will become a magnet for other likeminded people. You just have to get your message out there.

Creating a marketing message for the mass market tends to be so generic that it attracts no one. Products and services and innovation are generic too, they don't really do anything for anyone and they will most likely have nothing to differentiate from other businesses doing the same thing. So customers shop on price, which means the businesses make less money, customers get an inferior service and product and don't get the service they deserve.

Your why will help you develop your niche. Having a niche allows you to focus on one or a few sectors rather than the whole market. So you can tailor your message in your marketing, your services and products and innovation to be specific to your niche. This means only those people will respond to your marketing and those people will love what you do and how you make their life better. Everyone else will ignore you, which is what you want. You just want the people who get why you do what you do, to work with you.

As Simon Sinek says, 'People don't buy what you do; they buy why you do it. And what you do simply proves what you believe.'

It will also help you to differentiate your business from your competitors. This is a powerful tool for attracting the right type of customers and for pricing your services at the right price. And you want to work with people that feel the same as you; it makes life much more enjoyable and your work should be fun.

In fact I would suggest that you set your why as part of your criteria for accepting new customers and team members. Having the right people all around you is such a wonderful and powerful thing. It makes work fun because you all believe in the same purpose and you will share similar passions.

The values and principles of your business, the rules of the game for your business, will be fuelled by your why. These are essential to allowing your team to think for themselves but at the same time stick to the overall purpose of the business.

Your why will lead to your how and what you do, which you should start using in your marketing and when talking to people about your business. It gives a very powerful message that you stand for something and are working towards something great. The right type of people will relate to this and want to know more at the very least. These are the people that you want to work with, not the ones who don't share your beliefs and values.

If you lead with what you do and how you do it your message will sound no different to anyone else in your field of work and it doesn't create a compelling reason for people to listen to what you have to say. They will switch off before you can even get to your why.

You need to stand out from your competitors and this is one way of doing that.

Below are two messages to compare.

Message 1

"I'm a mentor and coach for entrepreneurs.

I have a seven step program that helps business owners create success."

Message 2

"I'm a mentor and coach for entrepreneurs.

I believe every entrepreneur deserves the right to fulfil their potential, be happy and do what they love.

You know how GPS SatNav in your car works out your current location, you enter where you want to go and then it works out the best routes? Well that's how I help entrepreneurs reach their ideal destination using the seven steps in The **PROFITS** Principles.

This is accomplished through educating, coaching and mentoring support, online and offline, to groups and individuals."

Which message resonated most with you?

Your why will give you, your team and your customers clarity of purpose. You and they will know exactly what it is you are striving towards and why. It will help you make tough decisions because if the answer doesn't align with your why or help you achieve your goals, to fulfil your why, then you won't choose that path. You will choose the option that does fit with your purpose. The same can be applied to how you spend your time. If you are spending time on tasks that are not linked to your purpose then you need to stop, delegate or outsource those tasks so you can instead focus your time on your purpose; your why.

Once you know your why and communicate it to others it allows you to start making a difference now rather than putting it off to fulfil later on in life, like most people believe and sadly never achieve.

You need laser like focus on where you are going, what you are doing and why you are doing it. Not only is it easier for you to do the right things in your business but it is easier for others to understand and for them to join you in your mission.

Having clarity means you will choose the opportunities that align with your purpose and every day you will work on only the things that will forward or enhance your purpose. Everything else will just be white noise that you can easily tune out and just focus on what is important to you and your business.

If you don't have this level of focus you will find yourself taking any path that is available to you instead of taking the path that best fits you and your goals.

EXERCISE

Schedule thirty minutes over the next week to sit down and answer the question 'why do I do what I do?' by either writing or speaking into a voice recorder on your mobile phone. In the first few minutes you may struggle or will only find a superficial answer but stick with it and keep talking or writing for the allotted time and you will find some real gold. Of course you will need to read or listen back a few times to mine that gold. The result is that you are a step closer to knowing your why.

Each of my businesses is fuelled by the same why, each business just helps in a different market or aspect of my why. My why is that no one should have to struggle to fulfil their definition of success in business, yet so many business owners struggle unnecessarily to keep their business going let alone work towards their goals. This happens for a number of reasons but I believe there are four key factors.

1. Not many people are taught entrepreneurship and business in school, I certainly wasn't, and society tends to steer us towards a 'safe' employee job rather than being an employer,

2. Planning and market research are often overlooked or not detailed enough,

3. There is little or no support, guidance and accountability,

4. The owners aren't passionate enough, if at all, about their business.

That's why I honestly believe that I am here on Earth to help these business owners with my gifts so they can lead a happier, more fulfilling and more authentic life. It is all achieved through education, training, coaching, mentoring and business support services. It's not only empowering business owners to help themselves but also makes a difference for the people and causes that they believe in. We each, one by one, can help to make the world a better place.

That's why I wrote this book to bring all of the **PROFITS** Principles together in one place where they can be understood and followed, so no longer do business owners have to struggle to 'earn a living' – they can actually realise their true potential, help make a difference and live their dreams.

You can download a free workbook to help identify your why from www.stevenbriginshaw.com/profitsbonus.

Make a difference today

Too often you will hear people saying "charity begins at home" or "I'll earn my money first and then help charities". Or you may hear someone say that they want to emulate Bill Gates and run a charitable foundation to help cure a disease or get rid of poverty.

As you will know the best time to help charities and causes close to your heart is today, not tomorrow. Sure, in the future when you have billions in the bank and a lot of time on your hands you will become an awesome philanthropist. But you can do so much right now to help people all over the world.

If you think about it, we live in a material world where most people are obsessed with owning lots of possessions and spending money on stuff they don't really need or want. They are good consumers collecting stuff to fill their homes, some stuff that may not be used again.

For example, I had a collection of over 1,000 DVDs and CDs. I didn't have enough time to watch them and listen to them all and at least 10%, most likely more, still had on the cellophane wrapper. Looking back now to when I had the collection I can see that I had a need to belong to something, to be part of something bigger than myself, which my collection superficially gave me. I was also a little materialistic. I thought that by having lots of stuff it would make me happy or successful. For a while I felt fulfilled but it didn't last long particularly when I had no room to store all of the films and music. After a while I realised that those films I didn't watch more than once and the music I didn't listen to again were paid with money I could have invested elsewhere and my energy used on making those purchases could have been used on working towards something more fulfilling. Yes I need to have hobbies and interests and I love films and music but this was wasted time, energy and money.

Instead my energy and money could have been spent on donations to help children who suffer bereavement, to fund research into Alzheimer's, to end child poverty or simply to give clean water to a child. I'm not saying don't buy DVDs, music or books, etc. Just make a conscious decision before making a purchase that you are buying something that you will use more than once or get a lot of enjoyment from it otherwise it is a waste. If you are a movie fan why not join a film subscription service where you can rent any film of your choice and as many films as you want and stream it to your TV. The same for your music. Plus you will free up a lot more space in your living room.

The money and energy you save on not buying material, wasteful stuff can instead be used for good by supporting the causes close to your heart, the causes and charities that you believe in. That's just one way in which you can make a difference.

You can also support charities through your business by linking what you do to certain projects. For example for every email that you send you could give a child access to clean water for a day. Or for every referral that you receive you could give a child in poverty access to shelter for a month. And then you could start to link your services to different charitable projects that are close to your heart.

Buy1 Give1 (B1G1) is a partner organisation that helps bring charities and businesses together. The charities commoditise their work allowing businesses to give either as a transaction donation, as mentioned above with the emails, or as a one off impact donation. So instead of donating to build a new school, you can donate to buy ten bricks to build the new school. You get a sense that you are really helping to make an impact, contributing for good.

My coaching and mentoring business is a Life Partner at B1G1. Not only does this differentiate us from our competitors it allows us to make a difference to those that are close to our heart. And it allows our customers to give back too as we cannot do it without them.

When you give to a cause that you believe in or simply help to make life better for someone else it creates a warm and fuzzy feeling inside you. You feel happy and a sense of pride that you were able to help. It's a feeling that money can't buy. You have no agenda to gain yourself, you just want to help in that moment.

You may have read or heard that when you give without wanting something in return you do end up gaining something in your life. The Universe or whatever you want to call it sees that you are giving your time, energy or money to causes that you believe in and you get something else back in return. It could be that warm and fuzzy feeling or it could be the opportunity that you've been waiting for. Whatever it is, making a difference is the most important and wonderful thing you can do.

You can take this even further by always smiling, so those that pass you in the street, on the road or in the office will smile too, it often is contagious. Smiling is such a powerful and wonderful expression and it is great when people smile back at you. You helped to make a difference in that moment of time where they were happy to see you smiling and wanted to smile back. You too feel happy. Try it for a day and then before you go to sleep look back at what a great day you had. You will want to do the same the next day.

Making a difference is all about you helping to improve the lives of others but although charities and helping those less fortunate all over the world are a big part of this so too are your family, your team and your customers.

For your family, help to give them what they want from life and to make a difference to those that are important to them. This may mean that you get home at 5pm every weekday to have dinner with your family.

For your team, help them to have fun at work and enjoy their time with you, your customers and to make a difference to those that are important to them.

For your customers, help them by providing services that will change their lives by solving problems in new and unique ways and to make a difference to those that are important to them.

You don't have to make a difference with your money. You can use your time and energy or your skills to help people.

Making a difference for all of those in your life and for those causes that you believe in should be something that you do every day.

EXERCISE

Here are a few questions to help you understand how and where you can make a difference for yourself and for others.

- *What causes, charities or projects do you currently support or would like to support?*
- *What upsets you or gets you angry?*
- *If you had a magic wand what would you change to make your world a better place?*
- *What are the things, regardless how small, you can do every day to make your world a little better for you or for someone else?*

Real world thoughts

Of all the **PROFITS** Principles this chapter is the hardest. You have to be brave and look within yourself. Learn more about yourself and love yourself for who you really are with all of your perceived positives and negatives.

If you are like me you may shy away every now and again from working on yourself because you know it is hard work and because you know at some point you will find something that you don't want to know about yourself.

It's only natural to fear what you don't know or to resist change and you will meet plenty of obstacles as you go deeper and deeper to your core essence. Learning more and more about yourself as you peel back the layers of the onion and develop, grow and evolve into becoming your true self.

But until you know who you really are and accept and love yourself for who you are then you will not be able to use your talents to fulfil the reason why you are here on Earth. Have confidence that any obstacles, fears and resistance can be worked through when you work on yourself and shining the light directly on them.

For me this has been the hardest part of my journey so far. Facing up to who I am and what I am here to do instead of who I was parading as.

I've always been able to fit in with the crowd. I was relatively popular at school and I was able to get along with the kids who were keen to disrupt the class, the kids who were keen to study and most kids in between. This happened because I changed myself to fit my environment, sometimes being myself but sometimes being another persona, which depending on your view may or may not be required at school.

I found myself doing the same thing through my career. Being able to change who I am to suit who I am communicating with.

I thought being able to get on with everyone was a strength but now as I am more and more my authentic self I can see clearly what was happening; I was being fake at times to satisfy the other person's needs or perceptions instead of just being myself all of the time. I was parading as another persona.

I discovered through working on myself that my behaviour stemmed from me wanting to be liked by everyone. For me it was a great feeling to be liked by lots of people and rubbish when someone didn't like me. But in the long run if I had continued being that way people would have seen through my act and realised I was a fake person, having too many personalities and traits to be genuine.

My ego was getting in the way because it was telling me that I could control what other people thought about me. It made me believe that I could make them like me, which without a Jedi mind trick I clearly can't do.

Now I am my authentic self as much as possible and I'm regularly working on being 100% authentic all of the time.

A result of being truly authentic is there will be people who absolutely love you and everything you do, there will be those that really dislike you and everything you do and those who don't really care either way.

If you are being your authentic self and people love you for who you are then there is no need to act like someone else or be a fake persona. The people that really get you believe in the same things and act in the same way. You will have great connections and build a great community with those people. How cool is that!

There will be those who really disagree with who you are and what you do but that is cool too. First of all my view is that everyone is entitled to their opinion, even if you don't agree with it, and if you don't you can choose not to accept it. Second there will be more people that love you than those that really dislike you. Third you choose whether to hang around with the people who get you for who you are, or the people who dislike you for who you are.

The people in between that don't really care either way are great news too as they will self select themselves out of your market. In other words, by being your authentic self you create your business niche because only those that really get who you are and what you are doing will buy from you, everyone else won't care.

It is possible that people that dislike you will buy from you to add fuel to their fire but you have a choice over who you work with and who you don't so you could choose to limit their fuel by not working with them.

The reason for starting my own accountancy practice, which I consider to be my first real business because it wasn't just a job with only me doing the work, was almost forced upon me.

I had the opportunity to buy in as partner at the firm where I worked, which was a dream come true for me. I had set a goal to make partner in the firm before I turned thirty when I joined as an eighteen-year-old trainee. I loved working there, most of the clients were great, it was close to home, the parking was great for access to the town centre and I really enjoyed working with the team there too.

But as it turned out buying in as partner wasn't a viable investment for me and my views of the future of the accountancy profession, where I wanted to take the firm, were different to those of the existing partners.

My dream was shattered and it left me with two choices. Stay as an employee with no more progression and see if in the future things change to make it viable for me to buy in, or start my own accountancy practice.

It didn't take me long to hand in my three months' notice and get my own business up and running, creating a new dream in the process.

Plenty of family and friends were worried about me taking that step to go it alone. Some even advised me not to do it, especially as Natalie and I found out she was pregnant with our first child in my final month at the firm. I knew, though, that this was right for me and because I loved business and entrepreneurship so much it was a perfect fit.

In summary, I started my accountancy practice, my first real business, to:
- Work for myself
- Get paid more as an owner rather than an employee
- Do something that I wanted to do within the profession – I wanted to take accountancy services to a different place than the partners at the firm where I was employed
- Make an impact on the lives of those I worked with and those causes I care about.

The businesses I started whilst still an employee at the accountancy firm, were started because I noticed an opportunity to help, I realised I had a skill set to do so, which was in an area I was interested in, and I wanted to make some money. These were remote bookkeeping and management reporting services and online marketing as an online retail affiliate.

Looking back, these were not really businesses, though, they were jobs I had created for myself. My why at the time was to help others and to get paid more.

The finer details of my why has changed over the years and I am sure it will evolve as I continue to change, but the core of my why has always been the same. In a nutshell, my core why is to help people with my skill set in the areas I love, while helping to make a difference to the causes that I am passionate about. It changed from fulfilling my why through an accountancy practice, to a bookkeeping and management reporting business to now, through my education, coaching and mentoring business.

I first started on this path of self-awareness when I worked with a professional coach to help me process the negative feelings and thoughts I was still experiencing from the death of my dad when I was four years old. It wasn't until I moved past those negative feelings and thoughts that I started to open up to be who I really am. I became self-aware and started asking questions about myself, which I had never asked before, and I was getting answers.

I still work with that coach to help me stay aligned to my true self and to understand who I really am and what I am here on Earth for. I meditate, write in a journal and speak aloud to Natalie to discover what I am really thinking and feeling.

I also work with business coaches and mentors where they ask me the hard questions and hold me accountable to finding the answers and delivering on what I find. All of this is to help me to dive deeper into my understanding of my why as it and I evolve.

Once you start down the path of self-awareness there is no way back. Taking the self-awareness path means you will need to continually work on yourself for the rest of your life.

You can't become self-unaware. A bit like in the movie *The Matrix*, if you choose to free your mind from The Matrix by taking the red pill then there is no going back. Sure, you can ignore the thoughts and feelings you have but that potentially could be harmful to you, and stop you from fulfilling your potential of making an impact in this world.

The question to ask yourself first before starting this journey is: 'Do I want to simply go through the motions of my existence reacting to the outside world, or do I want to be who I am supposed to be and bring my talents to help the world?'.

CHAPTER SUMMARY

Key points

- Being your authentic self is accepting yourself for who you are, operating in your natural flow doing the things you love and having fun.
- Accepting yourself requires you to acknowledge the 'negative' side you see or feel about yourself and asking yourself questions about what that feeling is trying to help you achieve.
- Getting clarity on your why will help you make decisions about what you do and what you don't do.
- Your why will attract the right customers, team members and opportunities to you because they will believe in the same big message that you do, you just need to put it out there.
- Your why will help you to develop your niche and will differentiate your business from your competition.
- Give back today to the causes, charities or projects close to your heart. Don't wait for tomorrow.

Exercise checklist

☐ *Find your favourite hobby and decide if you will go big on it*

☐ *Write down why you started your business*

☐ *Find what your why is, what you enjoy and what is your passion*

☐ *Write down 'why do I do what I do'*

☐ *Write down how and where you can make a difference today*

☐ *Get the identify your why workbook at www.stevenbriginshaw.com/profitsbonus*

SUCCESS LEAVES CLUES

There are plenty of successful people in business all over the world. You will find that the common trait is that they think the right way and get the right things done. Just by looking at what they do and how they do it you will see clues of how you can apply their approach to your business. Success does leave clues. It gives you an idea that if you can apply the same principles and approach to your business then you will have some success too.

Some ideas or principles may not transfer directly into your business so the key question to ask yourself is, 'how can I apply that to my business?'

Below are twelve success rules that will help your business and you to enjoy life; they certainly helped me. You don't need to adopt all of them but the more you do adopt the more successful you will be.

1. To create a business that can run without you

Your aspiration as well as every other business owner should be to create a profitable business that can run without you.

You can then use your time as you see fit to pursue hobbies, spend time with family, travel and create the lifestyle you have always wanted, while the business provides you with the personal income to do all of those things. And of course you can spend as much time in the business as you want but it is your choice rather than the business dictating when and where you have to work and what you work on. You just do the bits that you find fun.

Otherwise, you have just created a job for yourself. Depending on the work that you outsource or delegate you may have created a job from hell because not only do you need to deliver the services provided by your business but you also have to deal with the finances, the bookkeeping, the administration, the telephone, the marketing, find new customers, keep existing customers happy, manage the team, lead the team, etc.

If your main ambition is not to have a profitable business that can run without you then you are not a business owner. You are a job owner, which is right for some people but as you're reading this book I would say owning a job is not right for you.

The only time you will be a happy job owner is if the business is a hobby and you have plenty of time to do what you want outside of the business and the business can maintain the income that you desire. In other words, you can still go away on holiday each year, have four weeks off and carry on with the business.

But at some point you would have been a job owner and you are now on the trail to becoming a business owner. In fact your journey to becoming a business owner is detailed in the Entrepreneur Work/Life matrix below.

Single role	Employee	Business Owner
Multiple roles	Job Owner	Entreprenur
	Reliant on you	Not reliant on you

You will have no doubt started in the left upper corner of the matrix. You were an employee, working for someone else completing a single role within a business. You were earning a living working for someone in one of the other three categories on the matrix.

Then you decided to start a business, moving to the bottom left corner of the matrix, maybe to be your own boss, earn more money or to make a difference but you now had to do everything in the business. The sales, marketing, administration, bookkeeping, finance and delivering your service.

You became a job owner, which looks like a consultant, freelancer, coach, trainer or another self-employed role where you do the majority if not all of the work. You created a business that totally relied upon you, you created a job for yourself. If you don't work you don't get paid.

And now you are working towards the upper right corner which is a business owner. A business owner has a business that is profitable and can run with or without the owner, who chooses what they do. The owner only works on the things they enjoy and has one role within the business, because they have a team who uses well written systems to take care of the other functions.

The final destination, if you should choose to travel there, in the bottom right corner, is to be the owner of multiple profitable businesses that can run without you. You then become an entrepreneur.

You may be somewhere on that journey towards the upper right corner to becoming a business owner. Each day you should be working towards moving one step closer. Following the process in this book will help you complete that journey.

The left hand side of the matrix represents working for a living, where you have to work to live. The right hand side of the matrix represents living for work, where you choose what you do and love doing it.

EXERCISE

Here are a few questions you can ask yourself. If you answer 'yes' to every question then you are a business owner. If you answer 'no' to any question then this is an area you need to work on to help you become a business owner instead of a job owner.

- *Is your business profitable after deducting what you pay yourself?*

- *Does your business provide you with the personal income you need to fulfil your desired lifestyle?*
- *Can your business not only survive but actually grow if you were on a twelve week holiday without any contact?*
- *Do you really want to be a business owner?*

To stand any chance of creating a business that can run without you the systems mindset, which is the realisation that your business is just a collection of systems and people, is crucial. The systems and subsystems guide the people, so they can get the same great results, every single time, in every area of your business.

I started my entrepreneur journey when I was still an employee at an accountancy practice and created businesses on the side in my spare time. My online affiliate business was a hobby that I enjoyed which just happened to make a bit of money each month. My bookkeeping business was a job. Technically I was an employee and a job owner.

My bookkeeping business evolved into an accountancy business and, when I discovered it was not viable to buy in as partner at the accountancy practice where I was an employee, I stepped instead into my own business, full time. Now I was just a job owner and a very busy one I would become.

Learning through making mistakes, asking questions and implementing better practices, I figured out what I needed to do to get my job to become a real business and worked towards it. It just so happens that I fell out of love with that business before completing the journey, and sold it instead of continuing.

I used all that I had learned, though, to create (from day one) a business that can run without me. I became a business owner from scratch instead of owning a job first. This was the new bookkeeping and management reporting business I created shortly before I sold my accountancy practice.

We had a team in place from day one, we pre-sold the customers before starting the business, and the majority of the processes, or at least an outline in some areas, were written before any work was started. That was pretty cool!

2. Habits and rituals

Rituals are about paying attention to what's around you in that moment in time, what you are doing and where you are going. We live in a time pressured world where everything is at 100 miles an hour.

By slowing down for your rituals you can appreciate life for what it is in that moment and evaluate what is really going on in your life and your business. You can really get pleasure from and appreciate life at the slower speed, which will make you happier, allow you to have more focus and get more of the right things done. You may have heard the saying stop and smell the roses, this is exactly what rituals allow you to do.

By having this approach it will lead to harmony in all areas of your life because you will be aware of what is happening. You will understand and be aware of the things going on in your life; your business, family, wealth, health, friends and community. This is why having the right mindset is so important.

The good habits part is to make your rituals part of your daily life. Having good habits of rituals each day, week, month and year, helps you slow down to appreciate the moment, which helps you speed up your work towards your goals and make life more enjoyable.

Some rituals you may like to start with are:
- Gratitude, showing your thanks for anything in your life at that moment in time.
- Happiness, acknowledging what you have in your life that makes you happy.
- Meditation, clearing your mind and slowing down to align and connect with yourself to allow your intuition to come through.
- Planning, scheduling your day so you know exactly what you are going to do and when, which include the most important tasks that work towards your goals.
- Writing, keeping track of your thoughts, ideas and feelings in a journal, book or blog to get everything out of your head and on to paper to help you gain clarity.

Here are the rituals that have become good habits in a typical day in my life:

I start the day with spending time with my young daughter talking about the day ahead and having fun before our day starts. After breakfast, a shower, dressing, then I meditate for ten to twenty minutes and immediately write down the answers to eight questions I had written the night before. The questions are from Roger James Hamilton's Millionaire Master Plan.

Here are those eight questions from Roger James Hamilton:

1. What am I grateful for?

2. Who do I love?

3. Why am I so happy?

4. What am I committed to?

5. How committed am I?

6. What is my intention?

7. What is my wish?

8. Why am I here?

I then write in my journal for half an hour or so, before starting on the most important tasks of the day, the tasks that will move me towards my milestones. I stop for lunch around the same time each day and make sure I eat away from my work environment without distractions of mobile phones, the internet or the television. Other tasks that I need to do that day fit in before and after lunch.

My work finishes with me spending half an hour reviewing how my day went. I write down a few more things I am grateful for and what I have achieved during the day, giving myself a pat on the back. I then plan my next day, the bulk of the tasks were planned the month before, and write down those eight questions for me to answer tomorrow.

The gym is my next destination for weight training before a shower and dinner with my family. Family time, relaxing or social time follows, with more meditation before bed.

During my day I take two or three breaks of ten to fifteen minutes. I leave my mobile phone in another room on flight mode and only activate it when I need to use it. I only check my emails every other day because my team does that for me. The days when I do check my emails I make sure that it's not at the end or the beginning of the day. I never check my emails on my mobile phone.

Distractions like emails, phone calls, text messages, instant messages, social media notifications and surfing the internet will kill your productivity. From concentrating on a task to being distracted and then trying to concentrate back to where you left the task takes up a huge amount of energy and additional time. Only do these things when you have them planned in. If your role is to reply to emails instantly or respond to social media then this is not a distraction for you and will be a big part of your planned day.

This helps me to get loads done; I feel happy, I'm in my natural flow and I am working towards my milestones each day. Not every day is perfect and sometimes things don't go as planned, particularly if I miss one of my rituals, but the key is to stay relaxed and get back to your plan and your rituals.

Download the mp3s I use to meditate if you want to start or get help with meditating from www.stevenbriginshaw.com/profitsbonus.

3. Make work fun, in fact make your life fun

Let's face it, if work was boring and made you unhappy you would have no motivation to go to work and face your team and your customers. You would probably have a bad relationship with your team so their output would be poor as well as their customer relationships. And your customers will most likely be BMWs, Bitchers, Moaners and Whiners, because through having an unhappy and boring environment you have attracted the wrong people to your business.

By making it fun, your business will be more enjoyable to you; this will help you get out of bed in the morning. Your team will feel the same way, be self motivated, and love working with you and your customers. They'll create fantastic results and a winning customer experience, so that they will be grateful to work with you and your team, will pay a premium to do so, and share the same values and beliefs as you. The more you, your team and your customer have fun the more successful you, your team and your customers will be. Win, Win, Win.

Take having fun into the other areas of your life because just having fun at work and in no other area of your life would not be fun.

Wouldn't life be better if you had at least one more fun thing to do each day? Of course it would.

Your version of fun will most likely be different to someone else, so take the time to understand what it is and how to bring that into the business, while complementing your team members' version of fun too.

EXERCISE

Here are some questions to help you start thinking of things that are fun to you. To help get more fun in the business, have a brainstorming session with your team or someone external to your business, and ask these questions.

- *Throughout your childhood up to being eighteen years old, what things did you do that were fun?*
- *What fun things do you do now?*
- *What fun things can you do with your family?*
- *What fun things can you do on your own?*
- *What is currently fun in your business?*

4. Focus on results not the methods

You will have seen it yourself or know someone who works in an environment of input rather than quality output. The boss will want you to be sat at your desk from nine-to-five and not by the water cooler or chatting to your colleagues, regardless of the work you have done. They want you to stick to your hours each week even though you have found a more efficient way of doing things. With this environment you are unlikely to tell anyone how the improvements you have made can save time for others and make more money for the business. You, your colleagues and the business all lose.

By focussing on the results it doesn't matter how long it takes, unless there is a deadline, as long as it gets completed with the right outcome. This encourages innovation, autonomy and a trusting environment. It brings its own rewards too as you may have found a more efficient way to produce your work so you can use your now spare time to do something else. You could take that time off to do something that you enjoy or work on another project. You will also be happier to share your new efficient way of working with your team because it will mean faster and better results for your business and more time available to them.

You may be feeling that you would just find more work for them to do rather than give them time off. But if they have produced the results that they were asked to do in a quicker time than you expected then don't you think your team deserve a reward? If you don't, then you are still thinking with the input mindset.

What you could do with those Friday afternoons, because your team will love working with you and find it fun, is have a brainstorming session on how to improve other areas of the business or how to take the customer experience to a whole new level. You will focus on the ultimate output and results and then how to create them.

This is very similar to working smarter rather than harder. Yes you still need to work hard but work hard on the smart things, the things that will get the biggest progress towards your milestones for the least effort. You shouldn't work long hours but work on the tasks that get you the most results for the least hours required.

5. Split your income 70:10

It's unlikely that you were taught at school how to handle money – cash, credit, running a house and running a business. I certainly wasn't. You may have had to rely on the people around you and they may also have had to find things out for themselves. It is likely you will have some great money habits and a few bad ones.

The world we live in is driven by consuming and materialism. Credit is still easily available, not just from the banks but from pay day lenders, credit cards and store cards. Consumerism and credit fuel each other, encouraging you through the media to buy stuff and to pay on credit if you don't have the cash to pay now. You may be wise to this and only buy what you need and never pay for something unless you have the means to do so but the impulse purchases and desire for more things are difficult to avoid and control.

Typically for most people I know, and I used to be there myself, your money comes in to your bank account and then the money goes out. You may save some, one of the great money habits, but mostly the money goes on the cost of living, your lifestyle and repaying any debt.

Instead you can live by the 70:10 rule, it's actually 70:10:10:10.

This means you will:
- Save 10% of your income and never touch it until you stop having an income,
- Save 10% to invest as you see fit, so maybe a high interest bank account if you are against risk or buy some stocks and shares if you have an appetite for trading and higher risk, but it is yours to play with,
- Donate 10% to charities or projects that you believe in and want to help,
- Spend 70% on your lifestyle, repaying debt and having fun.

Not only will you have peace of mind that you have money behind you if something should go wrong with your business, but you will have a great sense of pride and happiness that you are able to help those that you feel passionate about.

The 70:10 rule is an ideal rule not a prescriptive one. The more of the rule you can follow the more peace of mind and gratitude you will have but doing a 90:10 is still better than spending 100% or more of your income.

Sometimes you will need to bend or change the rule depending on your circumstances but the key is for you to have understanding and some control over your spending and your spending should be less than 100% of your income.

If you are living a lifestyle where you spend 100% or more of your income then you have three options to get your lifestyle spend down to the 70%:

1. Come up with a figure from what you think is ok for you to spend off the top of your head for all the areas where you spend money. This could be grocery shopping, meals and drinks out, hobbies, home running costs, club subscriptions, running your car etc. Then once you have the amounts written down for each area review where you are spending your money so you can compare the actual to your expectation and ask yourself why you are spending the amount that you are. Do this for a three month period so you can get a sense of your spending habits. Then cut back where you feel you have been excessive. Be careful though, don't cut back and make your life miserable. Make sure that you can still enjoy the things you love. If you like working with numbers you can create a budget for your personal income and work out your ideal spending habits.

2. Earn more money. Pay yourself more money from your business, in the most tax efficient way, but only if the business can afford to do so. Work out how much extra you will need and update your business cash flow forecast to include your new personal income. Can your business afford it? If yes, please don't leave un-required cash in the business as you will find a way to spend it, so pay yourself more. If not, then focus on improving the profit in your business. You can focus on profit improvement in a later chapter.

3. Do both, cut back where you have been spending too much and pay yourself more from your business.

An initial step is to just start saving something, even as little as £10 per month. Don't think, 'I won't bother saving £10 as it's too low', just start saving it. This will get you into the great habit of saving and you can build up to 10% of your income from there. Then do the same for the investing 10%. Then for the giving 10%. Or do it in whatever order you want to or maybe all three at once. However, you can start giving immediately to those causes close to your heart or to your community by volunteering, giving your time for free.

You will need to master your personal finances before you can create sustainable financial success in your business.

Going back to the second point, you should pay yourself, tax efficiently, all of the money in your business current account, that doesn't need to be in the business, so you can save or invest it to create more assets to produce you more income. Make sure you have funds in the business that allow you to manage the day to day transactions. Have some funds available for new projects and a reserve if something goes wrong, say at most two to three months' worth of your monthly expenditure. If you keep it in the business bank account, you'll only spend the excess money on things you and the business don't really need.

I found the 70:10 rule really hard to start with but when I reviewed my spending I realised I was spending more money than I needed to and I found money to save and give to things I believe in.

I could see that I could cut back on things such as dining out and drinking so often when there was plenty of good food at home, and betting on football results in a vain effort to win money.

With the extra funds available I set up a monthly transfer to my savings account and I set up a monthly standing order to give as much as I thought was fair to charities that are close to my heart. It wasn't anywhere near to the 70:10 rule but it was much better than spending 100% of my income. It gave me confidence about my financial situation and made me feel good that I was helping to make a difference to those charities, regardless of how small.

The interesting thing is for me the 70:10 rule started to gain momentum and when my businesses were making more money I would pay the extra profit to myself and save or invest it helping to build up more personal wealth and confidence. I still do that now.

6. Having an open mind is essential to get what you want

If you think and do what you've always done you will always get what you have always got. In other words, if you want different results you need to think and do something different.

Who you think you are, what you think and what you do will always equal what you have. This is because you act like who you think you are and will get the results of that mindset.

To be a successful business owner you may need to think and act differently than how you think and act now. This change and adaption will most likely happen throughout your entrepreneurial journey and you will continually evolve as a person.

Too often you will see that people are busy doing all the time and not taking the time to think and act differently. They are getting loads done but it is not necessarily the right things to get their ideal future. They don't stop to think about their mindset or who they need to become to achieve their goals. They're not working in their flow and playing to their strengths, being their authentic self, which makes life harder for them than it needs to be.

To truly be a business owner you need to think, act and work like a business owner. If that is too much a step or not entirely possible for you right now then simply prioritise two or three business owner tasks before completing your other tasks. This will help you move closer to being a true business owner.

So what needs to change either in your mindset and education (Be) or your actions (Do) to get you what you want (Have)?

One thing you can do is to start with your ideal Have, your finished business, and work back to understand who you must be and what you must do to achieve that. Or add an extra zero to the end of your current annual turnover and profit. What sort of person will you need to be and what do you need to think about if your business was in that situation? What would you need to do differently compared to now?

Another thing you will need to do is to let go as your business isn't all about you and your ego. Yes the business will have your personality, your beliefs and values but your business is a living breathing thing on its own. Don't be the hero trying to do everything in your business. Simplify, automate, delegate or eliminate. Step back, trust and empower others to do it for you and with the knowledge that they will most probably not do as great a job as you but that's ok. Good enough is fine. Stop being the bottleneck in your business and start making real progress.

Have an open mind. Things may need to change, new ideas need to be objectively reviewed and so too current services/products. Be open to suggestions and ideas and be open to making the necessary changes in yourself to get your ideal Have.

Having a positive attitude is great but you also need positive action.

You will face change and challenges in your business, and in life, every day and it is how you react to those challenges and change that will determine your success. You cannot merely think about a positive thought you have to action it.

Your business will need to change just to keep up with an ever changing world. So to get ahead of the game you will want to embrace change before it happens and constantly challenge yourself. These are things that you will feel very uncomfortable with but it is only when you step outside your comfort zone that you and your business will grow.

Get feedback from your customers, check out your competitors, look at leaders in other markets and encourage innovation from your team to research what else you can do to improve. The research may make you feel uncomfortable but it will raise your game and potentially deal with any challenges before they arise. Remember, if it were easy everyone would be doing it.

7. You are responsible for everything

Everything that happens in your business is your responsibility. There are no outside influences, only the way you adapt and react to them. You have complete control of what you choose to do.

You make many decisions and choices every day, some more important than others but you are always deciding and choosing. You choose whether to have coffee or tea, eat at one restaurant over another, work with a customer or not, hire a team member or not, drive to work or walk. You may feel like some choices and decisions seem like they are imposed upon you like you wouldn't choose to walk twenty miles to and from your customers because driving there and back will be much quicker and your time is very precious. If you had nothing else to do that day and wanted some exercise then maybe you would walk the twenty miles. Either way you still make a decision, you choose regardless of how imposed or obvious it may seem.

In other words you are responsible for the decisions you make and therefore the choices you make.

If your business is profitable, it's because of the choices you previously made. If your business is loss making, it's because of the choices you previously made. If you have a great and happy team, it's because of the choices you previously made. If you have an underperforming and miserable team, guess what, it's because of the choices you previously made.

The decisions you make and the actions you take determine what you end up with.

You may feel that the poor economy is to blame because no one is spending. Or the banks are to blame because they won't lend to you. Or your customers are to blame because they pay you late. These are all just excuses for not taking responsibility for yourself. The buck stops with you. These conditions apply to every business, not just yours.

In a recession other businesses have not only managed but they have thrived. Other businesses are being lent money by the banks to grow and invest. Other businesses have great relationships with their customers and get paid in advance. This didn't happen by chance, it happened because the business owners did something different.

You choose your customers, you choose what you sell, you choose the price, you choose how your business runs and you choose your team. These are all based on the decisions you make.

If you take ultimate responsibility for your current situation you can then start to work out how to improve your situation.

Don't get stuck on the fact that it is your responsibility or your choice, focus instead on how can you improve it. What can you do differently to get a better result? If you continue to do the same thing you will always get the same results.

8. Spend your time with the right people

You are a product of your environment so be careful who you spend your time with. They have an influence on you, as you do on them.

If you are in a group of high achievers, you will also achieve highly. If you are in a group of people who want to mess around you will also mess around. This is really common in school where the environment and peer pressure play a huge part on what you do. As humans we have a sense of wanting to belong, to fit in with those around us.

Be careful who you spend your time with because they will influence you. You don't have to cut them out of your life – just be mindful of their impact upon you. Instead spend your time with people that inspire you and those that you feel are already successful. Listen to them and learn from them so that you too can inspire others and be seen as successful.

I'm more aware than ever about being around the right people, particularly people I want to learn from – not just in business but in other important areas of my life like parenting, self-awareness, music and health.

The people I tend to spend most of my time with, support me for who I am and as a minimum keep me at my current level while I learn from them to help me grow.

I limit, to a minimum, the time I spend with people that I don't resonate with or who I feel bring me down energetically or emotionally. This can be hard when they are part of your family or close friends but if they don't take your lead by being around people who can support them and learn from, then you should limit your exposure to them.

Someone close to me has a particular outlook of the world and of their self. I have encouraged them to be more positive and to love themselves more but it's something they need to do in their own time and of their own choosing, I can't make them do it. So when I see or speak with them and I catch them doing or saying something that brings me down, I call it out and ask them not to do it but instead talk about something they are happy about or grateful for. Slowly this may help them get to a better place but if they didn't follow my lead when I call it out, I would have to spend even less time with them.

9. Use hard facts

The key to making the right decisions for your business is to base your decisions on hard facts. Facts are black or white, there is no grey area. The numbers in your business are hard facts and if you are not already doing so you should be reviewing the key numbers, financial and non-financial, at least monthly to make sure you are making decisions on the hard facts in your business.

For example if you see your costs are higher than your income you know you are losing money, so you cut your costs or increase your income. If you see that feedback for your team for the month is seven out of ten and it's usually a nine, you know you need to improve it.

I previously helped a client identify, which of the services provided by his business were the most enjoyable to him, and which were the most profitable. Once we both understood what services he really wanted to work on and the level of profit each service contributed to the company, we could then easily see which services should be dropped because they were not profitable and not enjoyable, which services were outsourced because they were profitable but not enjoyable, and which services he spent his own time on because he enjoyed them and they were profitable.

It's simple, isn't it? Simple decisions become clear once you have the hard facts of the situation.

Sometimes the hard facts will be something you may not want to know and you may put off reviewing the facts because you have a gut instinct that already says things are bad. For example you could be losing money in your business every month and just hope that it will turn around soon. This is where your emotions get in the way of making the right decisions based on facts. You may have too much pride or you are scared to find out the truth of the situation but when you do find out the facts it allows you to instantly make a decision to improve the situation. Knowing the facts, regardless of how hard the truth may hurt, is essential to making the right decisions.

Once the decision is made it is important to implement change or ideas as soon as possible to continue to build momentum and to actually get the change or idea implemented. The longer you leave it the harder it is to implement as new ideas and thoughts get in the way or you will forget about it all together. Your thoughts should inspire direct action and it's always better to act right away rather than leave it for tomorrow.

10. See opportunities in mistakes

The quickest way you or your team will learn is to make mistakes. You try something new, something doesn't quite work out, you learn from it, improve what you are doing and don't make the same mistake again.

By the way trying something new and exploring are fun once you get over the fear of it being different and support yourself by knowing if what you find doesn't work or isn't helpful you will simply learn from it.

The mistakes you and your team make are the natural innovation process for your business. Constantly trying new things and adapting the processes in your business to deliver the perfect system.

When mistakes do happen make sure you learn why the mistake happened and then ensure it doesn't happen again.

You will no doubt celebrate successes in your business like when you win a new piece of work, or hit the goals you set for your team or when you win an award. Celebrating what has been learned from your mistakes and the mistakes of your team is also a good idea.

It ensures that everyone in your business knows about the mistakes made and the learning that follows so no one will make the mistake again and the new learning is shared.

Also, you want your team to always try to improve things or try out new ways of working. Giving a degree of autonomy that is within your set guidelines allows for innovation to happen, particularly from the team who are on the front line.

I have a client that has a 'Wall of Fame' in a prominent place in their office so everyone in the business celebrates successes and learning from mistakes. It's a bit of fun, the team know what is and what isn't working, and learn from it.

11. Get external help and use experts

Have you ever spoken to someone outside of your business and they have either asked you a question or made a suggestion where you said to yourself, "Why didn't I think of that"? This is a picture of the obvious that you could only see through someone else's eyes.

If you have, it shows the importance of regularly speaking with and listening to someone outside of your business. Someone who has great knowledge of business and is skilled in an area that compliments your own.

If you haven't yet experienced that moment then find that someone so that you can ask yourself, "Why didn't I think of that?"

As the business owner you are too close to the business to sometimes see the obvious bigger picture. Having regular discussions with a mentor, coach or accountant will allow you to get an outsiders perspective who will give you an honest answer and ask the sometimes difficult questions that you will not ask yourself.

You will also get accountability from the outsider. They will hold you to your word, so if you say you will do something by next month they will make sure that you get it done. They are there to help if you get stuck or need a hand.

If you include the key numbers of your business in these sessions it will also make sure that you have actually prepared the numbers and you can also get help with understanding what those numbers mean. Then making the right decisions becomes easier.

Being a business owner is a lonely place, even if you have other directors or partners in the business. Having someone to talk to about your business, your ideas, to brainstorm or just to let off steam is a vital tool in your tool kit.

It's ok to ask for help, you can't do it all on your own. Humans are social beings so it will be more fulfilling to work with others towards your goals than on your own.

There simply is not enough time in the day for you to do everything in your business and you want to use your time as wisely as possible.

So when you work with suppliers make sure they are an expert in their field. Whether that is bookkeeping, administration or tax planning. You will then be able to rely on them to get the job completed when they say they will and the work will be to a high standard.

This will ensure that you spend your time doing the things that only you can in your business and more importantly you can do the things that you enjoy. You will get so much more done and have more fun.

The experts will handle their area, that's why they are experts. You can rely on them getting the end result that you want without any worry or input from you.

12. Do what only you can do

Your time is the most precious thing in your life and like many business owners you are most probably wasting time.

Wasting time by doing things in your business that someone else can do to get the same result. Missing out on spending time with your family or doing the things that you want and love to do. An example of some of the time wasting things are listed in the left hand column below and an example of some of the tasks you should be doing on the right hand side, but the lists are not exhaustive:

List of Low level tasks	List of business owner tasks
Bookkeeping	Strategy for the business
Answering the telephone	Marketing strategy
Selling	Training
Booking meetings	Innovation
Payroll	Leading
Filing	Managing
Answering your emails	Content creation

Other administration	
Social media posts	
Video editing	
Website analysis	
Website updates	
Marketing tasks	

Instead, to make better use of your time you should be spending your time in the business only on the things in the right hand column above. The things that only a business owner can do, no one else in the business is able to do it.

Then the time you have left over can be spent on what is important to you, like with your family, hobbies and interests and working towards your personal goals.

Depending where you are on your journey to business owner from job owner you may not be able to immediately stop doing all of the things listed in the left hand column but instead you should build the delegation or outsourcing of those tasks into your business goals. Focus on the most time consuming low level tasks first.

EXERCISE

Here is one very quick way to work out what you can delegate or outsource:
- *How much do you currently earn for the business each week (if you think in months then take your monthly income multiply that by twelve months and divide by fifty-two weeks)? Divide that by your hours worked each week. What is your hourly rate? Write it below.*
- *Hourly rate*
- *Now list the low level tasks you are currently completing.*
- *Now find out what low level tasks you are currently*

completing and find someone in your team or a supplier that can complete those services at a lower hourly rate. It makes sense doesn't it. If you can pay someone with a lower hourly rate than you to complete a task then you can focus on earning more money with the time you free up. In most cases, the people you give the tasks to will be able to complete the tasks in a quicker time too because they are good at it and enjoy it.

You will obviously need to make sure that the person taking on those tasks can actually get the right end result and if you have a particular process then you should have a system for them to follow.

Build a great team around you. This includes outsourcing, with each team member competent and responsible for their tasks. No one person can do everything so you will need different people for the different functions of your business.

You may feel that you enjoy and are best at doing some of the lower level tasks and don't enjoy some of the business owner tasks. If that is the case then you have two possible paths to follow, you either bring in a CEO to run your business and the CEO does the business owner tasks for you, which may involve you having to do the business owners tasks until you can get the right CEO, or you get a job doing the low level tasks as you may not have what it takes to be a business owner.

CHAPTER SUMMARY

Key points

- If you are serious about owning a business rather than just owning a job then you need to live for work and not work to live.
- Having good habits and rituals will help to create harmony and happiness in your life.
- Save, invest and give some of your income. Don't spend it all. Get as close as you can to the 70:10 rule.
- Be aware that in order to get the things you want you will have to change and be open to that change.
- You choose how you react to the things in your life. Take responsibility and choose to get what you want.
- Spend time with people who support you and from whom you can learn.
- Allow yourself and your team to make mistakes and celebrate the learning.
- Get help from outside your business to help you see the wood from the trees.
- Delegate or outsource the tasks you don't enjoy and as a business owner shouldn't be doing.

Exercise checklist

Write down questions about your current business to see where you are on the entrepreneur work/life matrix

Find out what is fun for you and your team

Work out what you can delegate or outsource

Get meditation mp3s at www.stevenbriginshaw.com/profitsbonus

YOUR IDEAL CUSTOMERS
Know Your Ideal Customer

You can't provide your services to every single customer in your market, and there will be some customer groups that you simply don't want to work with for one reason or another.

To attract every customer you will need to create a service and message that appeals to everyone. You will find this can only be done by creating a very bland and general message to ensure you don't alienate some customer groups. What will happen is that instead of the message appealing to everyone it will actually appeal to no one. So you will end up with very few customers and most likely customers that you ideally wouldn't work with.

Some customers will have different beliefs or values to yours, some won't pay the price you have set, some won't value your contribution and some won't pay you on time.

What you do, how you do it and why you do it will appeal to some but not all customers. So it's these customers that you should focus on and leave the other customer groups for someone else.

These customers will fully appreciate how you help them and share the same beliefs and values. They will understand why you do what you do and they will make working with them fun for you and your team.

You will go inch wide and mile deep, giving great content and value for a select and exclusive group of customers. Rather than mile wide inch deep, giving a tiny amount of value to a huge audience of customers.

You will create a club of customers who think the same as you, value the same things, appreciate your help and who will want to buy from you again and again.

You know what makes your customers tick, the problems they face and the kind of solutions they look for, so you can market to them extremely effectively. This means your message will hit home for each customer because they all think the same, want the same and have the same problems. So if they are in a position to buy from you they will, and if they are not they will try to move things around so they can.

This makes creating marketing content much easier because you only have one customer type in mind when writing it and it only needs to appeal to one type of customer. The great thing about this is that all of the potential customers that aren't ideal for your business will disqualify themselves because the message doesn't appeal to them. So you only spend time with your ideal customers and not customers who are less than ideal.

You will also be in a great position to actually come up with even more great services to solve their problems because you will be so tuned in to what they need help with. You will have them in mind for every new service and when you are writing your marketing copy.

Getting your message out will also be simple because you will know where your customers hang out. Do they use Twitter, Facebook, Google, magazines, networking groups, national memberships etc.? So you can send out your message using the right media where all of your ideal customers will read it and then follow your call to action.

You will also be able to exactly explain who you work with when discussing your business with someone you haven't met before, so they will instantly be able to understand if they are your ideal customer or if they know someone else who you can help.

Creating your ideal customer starts with your Why, because you want to work with people who have the same values and beliefs as you. Once you understand that you can then focus on a particular industry or sector or gender or business, etc. that you enjoy working with, can help the most, or which will be happy to pay a premium for the value that you can offer them.

When you are doing this try to put a name to a face, create a persona or think of someone you already know, so that you can see their face every time you write marketing copy or create new services. Once you have their face and name, create a back story so that you know all the facts about them. Where do they live? What's the marital status? Do they have children? Do they drive? What are their hobbies etc?

EXERCISE

Below are a few questions that will help you get started to work alongside your why from the earlier chapter.
- *Who are your best customers and why?*
- *Do you already have two or more customers with the same background, industry, sector, attributes etc?*
- *What types of customers are best suited to your skills?*
- *Who do you most enjoy working with and why?*
- *What are your interests and hobbies?*

You can create a profile of your customers by looking at their gender, age, location, hobbies, what they buy from you, what industry they are in etc. Also by asking yourself: what are their goals, why they haven't achieved their goals, what are their problems, what do they desire to solve their problems, what questions do they search for on the internet, what are their emotional needs and what are their buying preferences.

This will lead you to understand your ideal customer and help to create a niche, a certain group of people you will only work with. Also think about who you enjoy working with the most, what are their personality traits and profile, which will give you clues to your ideal customer profile. All of the knowledge about your ideal customer flows into your marketing plan.

It is ok to say 'no' to a customer that doesn't fit your ideal customer profile, in fact you must say 'no'. If they do not tick all of the boxes then it is likely they will become a customer who requires more of your time, doesn't fit in with your other customers, makes life difficult for your team, won't pay your invoices on time.

The monetary gain from taking on a non-ideal customer will be outweighed by the extra time, effort and energy required to service them.

This extra time effort and energy should instead be best used to help service better your ideal customers or used to find more of them.

There are always more ideal customers out there, you just need to look in the right place and have the right message.

An ideal customer for my coaching and mentoring business is someone who is in business already, effectively selling time for money as a professional or practitioner (like a coach, therapist, consultant, accountant etc) who is ideally working in health, finance or technology (these are the sectors I love the most). They will have hit a glass ceiling or plateau and either can't seem to get any more money into the business or they can't seem to find the time to do anything else. This could be someone working on their own (a job owner) who has a five figure business and wants to get to six figures, or it may be someone with a small team who has a mid to high six figure business and wants to get to seven figures.

The reason customers buy from you

The main reason customers will buy from you is because you offer a solution to their problem or a result they want to achieve.

But your customers will also buy from you because they share the same passion as you for your why – they will have the same values and beliefs.

Also, you will offer customers something unique. This is your unique selling proposition (USP), which will also be linked to your why.

The problems you solve, the results you achieve, your why, your values and beliefs and your USP are extremely important as the basis upon which to differentiate your business. You will attract the right customers and they will completely buy into what you do, how you do it and why you do it, which will lead to a very loyal customer base who will be happy to recommend your services to anyone they meet.

As you offer so much value to your ideal customers they will be willing to pay a premium price to work with your business and to get the customer experience you detail in your USP. In addition, because you have a premium price customers will think you must be good at what you do and will be happy to pay for it. And the more value you can offer to your customers at a low cost to your business the more profitable your business will be.

If you use a low price to differentiate your business from your competition then you will attract price sensitive customers. Customers that will leave your business as soon as they find someone cheaper. These customers are not interested in the value you provide, why you do what you do or what you believe. They just want the cheapest service and typically these are the people who are hardest to deal with and will take up the majority of your time. These customers are your BMWs – Bitchers, Moaners and Whiners.

So what is your USP?

A list of the problems and barriers your customers have will help you understand what your customers feel and what your business is up against. Use your team to help you brainstorm – their interaction with your customers will be a great insight.

Having a list of problems is just the surface level, you will need to go deeper, to an emotional level, to find out their pain, fears and frustrations; to really understand why the problem is so important to your customers and why it needs to be fixed.

You can speak directly to your existing customers when you next meet, or call, or create a feedback questionnaire.

EXERCISE

To help find your USP, you should put yourself in your customers' shoes and answer these questions.
- *What problems do they face?*
- *What are they trying to achieve and what is stopping them?*
- *What pain, fears and frustrations do you think your customers experience because of their problems and barriers?*
- *Contact your customers to ask these questions to get more insight.*

Let's take builders as an example to show what one of the problems you find could look like. You know how most people have an issue with builders because they never know what work is included in the price, which means that people worry about being charged extra and ripped off.

Just replace the word builders with your profession or sector and replace the problem and the pain with those that your customers feel.

Once you have the problems, their frustrations and their goals you can then work on solving them and how your services fit as part of the solution.

Explain what your service does to remove that pain so it is no longer a concern and barrier to your customers and explain the benefits that your customers will receive as a result.

Continuing with the example above let's look at what the solution and benefit looks like. Well what we do is to share our detailed plan and quote of the job with the customer, after a thorough survey, so they know exactly what work will be completed and what the price is for all of that work, which means that you can be certain that you will not pay a penny more for the agreed work.

Again, just replace the solution and benefit with your own.

After, create a sentence or two in plain English to explain each problem your customers face and the solution you provide, so it is easy for your customers to understand. When you have a list of these you can then work out which are the strongest USPs and use these or just one in your marketing. You may even want to shorten a USP to become a strap line for your business.

Make sure you communicate your strap line and strongest USPs to everyone that comes into contact with your business. Have them on your email footer, your letterhead, your website, your social media bios, your adverts, brochures, invoices, posters on the walls in your office and as many other places as possible.

Customer experience

The great service that you provide your customers is no longer enough, you now need to provide your customers with a great experience. Everything that you do must be with the customer in mind. From simple communications like answering the phone or sending an email to providing results they desire. In fact go above and beyond their expectations to under promise and over deliver.

It is not just about what you do but why and how you do it. There is an emotional connection with your customers and your business not just a transactional connection. So you will want to make sure that the emotions your customers feel are the right emotions such as happiness, gratitude and delight.

Giving a great customer experience is all about relationships. You want to create and manage a great relationship with every one of your customers, making them feel like they are your only customer. To do so you need to set the scene and meet your customers' expectations. Simply do what you say you can do and do it better or quicker or in a way that your customer will appreciate even more.

Communication is also key for a great relationship. Stay in contact with your customers. Give them the information that they need before your customers ask you for it in a format and language that they will understand and appreciate. Also keep them up to date on the work you are helping them with and get their involvement where it is relevant. Get feedback from your customers in a format that is easy for them to understand and use. Then make the changes they have asked for.

By having great customer relationships it will make you want to help your customers more and increase your love for what you do and why you do it. Not only will your customers really appreciate what you do for them, they will want to continue to work with you for as long as possible.

You may see or receive a great customer experience anywhere that you go or unfortunately you may see the opposite. Each restaurant you eat at you will be aware of the waiter or waitress that goes the extra mile to create a great evening for you. Or when you are next in a department store you will be aware of the sales adviser that asks you the right questions to help you choose what you want without you having to ask for help.

For example, visualise this when you arrive at your holiday destination. You are greeted by someone with a huge smile who welcomes you and walks you to the front desk, they discuss your holiday with you, ask great questions and listen to you. At reception you receive a glass of champagne to toast the start of your break. The receptionist has taken you through all of the key info of the hotel, you are given a personal tour of the resort for things to do, restaurants and shops to visit based on what is important to you on your holiday, all obtained from the driver asking great questions. During your stay the hotel staff learn your name, learn your favourite drinks, always smile, they make sure you are enjoying your experience as much as possible. You have Apple TV in your hotel room to play the videos from your iPad and iPhone on the big screen TV. The rooms are immaculately clean, there is no litter anywhere on the resort, the gardens and shrubs are beautiful. The beach and pools are always clean with plenty of soft cushioned sun loungers. This list goes on and on. But notice none of these things take a great deal of effort, just some thought, but they give you an experience you will never forget rather than just another holiday.

Your role as the business owner is to keep existing customers and win new customers. This should be one of the things that you work on each day.

So it is important that throughout your business you have the same approach to the customer experience in all areas where your customers come in to contact with you and your business. Your website will need to give the same message that you talk about, your team will need to interact in the same way with your customers as you do, the correspondence you send out to your customers' needs to follow the same message, how you deliver your end results needs to fit the same approach etc. For example you or your team wouldn't answer the phone using slang if you want to be seen as a professional business. Or you wouldn't present a report to your customers in a grotty folder if you offer a premium service. Every interaction with your customers needs to say the same thing about your business, whether it is that you are professional, high end, caring or have an eye for detail.

In making sure that you are doing the right things to keep existing customers and win new customers, getting their feedback on a regular basis is essential. When you understand what your customers want, how they feel about your services and your industry and what problems they face you can then make sure that you give your customers what they want, give them positive feelings and solve their problems. It sounds simple, and it is, but you will be one of very few businesses that get customer feedback and act on it.

How often you will get the feedback from your customers and potential customers depends on the number of times that they will interact with you. If you sell something once and have very little contact with your customers then you will want to get their feedback say twice a year. Once at the point of buying and then six months later when the work has been done and they are hopefully seeing the results. Plus this will keep your business in their mind if you don't already have an email and post newsletter or other forms of keeping in contact.

Or if you have an ongoing relationship where you speak with your customers on a monthly or quarterly basis then monthly or quarterly feedback is fine. Get your customers feedback on the frequency of the customer feedback. If you ask them if you are asking for feedback too much or not enough they will let you know.

Feedback can be gained through many different methods such as questionnaires, face to face chats, phone interviews and the Net Promoter Score. You will first need to know what you want to find out and tailor the questions appropriately. Closed questions that give a yes or no answer are best but when you are looking for inspiration or ideas then open questions will be ideal. Using a scale of one to ten is also a great method to use – always ask for an explanation for their answer if the score is eight or below and what can be done to make things even better.

From your own experiences of feeling completely looked after at a restaurant, shop or hotel you will have associated that feeling with attention to detail into the smallest things. They really do matter and that is the difference between a good experience and a great experience.

It is these tiny noticeable things that you will need to establish in your business so your customers see your attention to detail, are wowed by their impact and know they are being looked after to the best of your ability. They will really make a difference to your customers and how they feel and think about you and your business.

Have a brainstorming session with your team to work out what your tiny noticeable things are and when and how you should present them to your customers. Then make them happen and record the reactions from your customers. The next step will then be to systemise your tiny noticeable things so everyone in your team knows how to make them happen.

What you will find is that offering your customers the right service to solve their problems or achieve their desired results and giving them a great customer experience, will result in more profits for your business. Or to put it simply, more profits are a direct consequence of doing the right things in your business; more profits will just happen. With more profits your business will have more cash and as a result you will get more time through being able to get the right team around you. Money doesn't buy happiness but doing what you love, getting paid well and having time to do what you choose, will certainly make you happy. You will feel blessed, grateful, and appreciative of the great things you have in your life.

Become an expert in your field

By focusing on your ideal customers, your niche, delivering a world class customer experience and working in the areas of work that you love and that you are good at you will start to be seen as an expert in your field.

No one else will do the things that you do in your way and because of your attention to detail by knowing your ideal customer and how best to wow them, you will rise above the other businesses in your industry.

Being seen as the expert is a by-product, a consequence just like making more profits, of doing the right things for the people that you really care about.

You can do certain other things to help speed up the process of becoming an expert, like publishing helpful and valuable content for your ideal customers and nailing how you describe yourself and what you do that resonates best with your market. This will also help to raise your profile and get you known by more and more people in your niche.

By you becoming an expert in your field, area or industry you will be seen as the go-to person for the particular solutions you provide. Everyone will know you as that person, your reputation will precede you, so you will receive constant referrals and it will be clear to everyone what it is that you do.

What will happen is that your customers will come to you rather than you chasing for new customers.

When opportunities arrive you can also work in different niches of the market, if you want to, and can deliver the same great results. But to start with it is best to focus on one area to build your name and expertise.

This will also lead to you being able to charge a premium price for your services as you will be the expert and therefore your customers will willingly pay that premium.

Real world thoughts

I found it highly logical and understood why and how I needed an ideal customer but to just serve them, my niche, and no one else seemed very uncomfortable for me at the beginning.

I'm still not totally sure why I found it hard to choose a niche and work on my ideal customer. Maybe because I was scared of working with only a small section of the general population. By working on the process and regularly refining it I got over that fear.

Maybe I saw it as having a bigger pie to fight for; smaller pieces seems better because the pie is bigger. But the fight to get customers in a general market is so much harder. You could go days without eating but it's rationalised to be ok because the pie is bigger.

Having a bigger slice from a smaller pie and getting regularly fed is far better but seems scarier because the pie is smaller.

One way that helped me was to understand who I am and to then find people like me because I know that some of my best friends are similar to me and I enjoy spending time with them. I also want to enjoy spending time with my customers.

When creating your customer profiles for the first time you just have to go with your best guess at the time, like a stick in the sand. You can then change and improve it as you go but you have to start somewhere.

It's very liberating saying 'no' to customers that don't fit your profile and if you have the connections you can always introduce them to someone else who would like to work with them.

I've found that the people I have said 'no' to or that they aren't in the right place to work with me really value my honesty and in some cases it creates an even better relationship because of that.

A big trap is to not say 'no' because you feel it could be easy money. Don't chase the money. A few times a year I still have to hold myself back from taking work I perceive to be easy from non ideal clients. In the long run it ends up being harder work than you think and because deep down you don't really want to do the work with that customer it becomes a drag and the customer doesn't get the delighted service you would normally give to your customers.

These customers tend to demand more of you too so you may end up resenting them – but you decided to work with them so you need to help them and give them what they have paid for.

It's hard to put a value on your happiness, freedom, fun and enjoyment unless it is always at the forefront of your mind. That's why it's hard to turn money down because it is easy to put a value on it. It's printed on the currency, and there will be times when we could really do with the extra money, but having happiness, fun and freedom as a choice is way more valuable than some money, not to mention what could end up being a dissatisfied customer.

A USP is essential and for me I believe the USP for my businesses is grounded in my own experience and the content, like the **PROFITS** Principles, that comes from that experience. There is only one me in the world and that helps to differentiate my products and services, even though I don't deliver them all myself.

The little details are really important to me and when I've had a great experience at a restaurant, hotel, shop or event it tends to be those who have paid attention to the little details that I have enjoyed the most.

We always revisit our favourite hotel in Greece for family holidays simply because they really take care of the little details, as I described in this chapter. When we first went back we were worried whether we would get the same experience, thinking that it may have been a one off, but the hotel uses systems, gets the right people in the team (some are still there from when we first visited) and the right training to get the same great result every single time.

Sure, things have gone wrong, like one time in one of their many restaurants I felt my meat wasn't cooked correctly and didn't eat it. The waiter offered to have another plate brought out but I wasn't keen on eating anything else, but when we got back to our hotel room there was a large complimentary platter of buffet food and a bottle of wine there waiting for me because they knew I didn't eat my meal. We were so impressed not just with the thoughtfulness and kindness but also by the speed at which they had acted.

To them the delight of their customer really does come first.

They respond brilliantly to challenges and win even more hearts that way.

Another reason why they are so good at what they do is because they always ask for feedback from their guests and more importantly they listen and make changes. Just one example that I am aware of is when they heard from the guests that the pools were too cold in the cooler months, the next year they heated all of the pools.

CHAPTER SUMMARY

Key points

- To get your message heard it needs to be tailored to a specific market or niche.
- Go inch wide and mile deep, not mile wide and inch deep, for your chosen specific market or niche.
- Your marketing is easier when working with a specific market or niche that you know and understand.
- You choose your customers so choose the customers that are fun for you to help and say no to the customers who don't fit your ideal profile.
- Your customers will choose you over your competition because your why, values and beliefs match up with theirs.
- Competing on price is the fast lane to failure unless your perceived unique selling proposition (USP) is you are set up to do it cheaper than anyone else.
- Your USP will define your business and attract your customers. It will also be a part of you, as you are unique.
- The experience you provide your customers must be congruent throughout their journey and based on a great relationship.
- Simply by focusing on a chosen market or niche and by getting your content, story and experience out there you will rise as an expert in your field.

Exercise checklist

Write down who are your ideal customers

Find your USP from your customers' perspective

GETTING THE RIGHT TEAM
Recruit the right people

If you were recruiting a new team member you may follow this process. You would create a job spec or description based on the skills required to complete the role and advertise through online and offline publications or you would use an agency. You would then review the CVs received from the applications, or just the candidates the agency puts forward, and then interview them. After the interviews you will offer the job to the person who ticked all the boxes or had the best fit for your job description.

This is the way most businesses recruit and it is staggering to hear from business owners the amount of team members that do not last in their role for more than a year. In fact, I know people who see it as their duty to get new jobs every two to three years. In other words, these individuals have no care or consideration for the businesses they are working for. It is just a pay cheque to them.

Like everything in life, if you want different results you have to do something different. And you have to do something different to everybody else to get exceptional results.

An alternative is to recruit based on personality, motivation and beliefs and values first and then consider skills. Sure, there will be some personality requirements in the normal process but no questions around why they get up in the morning, what they believe in, what are their values.

The answers to these questions need to align to yours and those of your business, similarly with your ideal customers. When you have a team that believe in what you believe, they share the same values and feel they have the same purpose then they will have total buy in to your business. Especially if they are results focused, can follow processes and can think on their own to improve and create new systems.

They will understand your why and share it, they will be self motivated because they believe in what you believe and they will want to stay with your business for as long as it takes to fulfil their purpose and that of the business. Not only that they will have fun working with you and the rest of the team and work should always be fun for everyone involved. Isn't that more powerful than having a team member who has the right skills?

It is far more important to get the right people in your business than it is to get the right skill set. Skills can be taught if you have the right person to start with. You will find the right role for them if they fit well with your why.

By focusing on personality when recruiting your new team member, instead of skills, you will need to follow a different process than everyone else.

I have clients and friends who have held half day seminars as part of their recruitment process and at the seminars they talk about the business, their why, their vision, where their passion comes from, their values and beliefs and don't even mention the role at this point. Everyone who doesn't share the same view point can leave no questions asked. The people left are then those that share their values and beliefs and buy into their why. A perfect fit for a team member.

It's at this point that the role is explained and how this contributes to the overall vision of the business. Again, the candidates have the opportunity to leave if this is not for them.

At the same seminar the remaining candidates will complete a short questionnaire to ensure they have the right mindset and to assess what skills they currently have. Then they will complete a group exercise based around the role to see how they interact.

The seminar is finished with a questions and answers session from the candidates to the business owner and the candidates are asked to complete a feedback form, which also asks if they would like an interview for the role.

The individual interviews are then conducted to assess the personalities on a more personal basis after which the right candidate will then be offered the job. Doesn't that seem more fun for you and a better way to recruit the potential team members?

You may be asking 'how do they fill the seminar?' Well like with your ideal client where you know everything about them, where they hang out, what they read etc., you will also need to complete that exercise for your ideal team members.

You can then advertise the role in the right places and get the right people to come along. However, I know someone who has recruited a team member by experiencing their level of service as a customer. In this case my friend was a customer at a restaurant and he was so impressed with the attention to detail, the level of care taken and the conversation with his waitress that he decided to give her a job. So maybe there is an occupation that will provide your business with the right team members.

EXERCISE

Think of the role that you want to recruit for next, using the organisation chart exercise from earlier in the book, and answer the following questions to help you get the right person for the role.

- *How will you share your business vision to inspire a potential team member?*
- *What questions will you ask to ascertain if they share the same beliefs and values as you?*
- *What questions will you ask to understand if they will fit within the existing culture of your business?*
- *Where do your ideal team members hang out?*
- *Will you Google and check social media to see how your potential new team members act outside of work?*

Share knowledge and develop

When you have your team it is important to keep them up to date on how the business is performing in general and how it is doing compared to your goals. Your team bought into your business upon recruitment so they should be able to see how your vision is being fulfilled. Not only that they need to see how they are contributing to the business and the goals and if necessary how they can improve things.

Having a common purpose throughout the whole business will give greater clarity and purpose. Everyone will know what they need to do and why and they will go the extra mile to get it done if necessary.

Short monthly team meetings to give a progress update are a good idea. More frequent short meetings with top level management will most likely be required to keep on top of goals, opportunities, challenges and customer experience levels.

Also involve your team in helping you improve and create new services, work on how to create the best customer experience, how to improve the systems in the business or a better way of working towards business goals. Getting your team's input is essential as they are your eyes and ears of the business, they are on the front lines and have the most contact with your customers. Also getting ideas and feedback from more than one person will create ideas that you wouldn't have thought of on your own and they may be a better solution or result.

And remember you are all team members of the business, the team, and should be working together to support and help each other as well as play your part in achieving the goals of the business. Being part of a team is a winning mentality. On a football pitch there are eleven players on one team, each with their own role but they help and support each other throughout the game to win. If everyone wanted to score a goal the formation and tactics would be useless and the team would no doubt lose every match.

Labelling your team members as staff or employees creates a different mentality, an 'us and them' mentality, between your team and you and your management team. It creates a culture where it is harder to get everyone to pull in the right direction and to encourage openness. So be careful how you refer to your team. Regardless of the position of the people in my businesses, we refer to each other as team members. Like any other team, we all are aware of the team goal and work towards it as a team helping each other.

Always give your team the opportunity to add to their knowledge and skills. They will become better team members as a result and will appreciate the time and attention that you take with them to help them become better at their role and better as a person.

They will also be able to follow the same process as you by setting goals, planning, taking action, measuring and improving. This will help them to understand how you work and what brings you your success, and it will also give your team members great autonomy and responsibility for their section of the business.

There is a danger that by helping your team to become faster, leaner and stronger they could leave your business but if you have recruited the right people to start with it will dramatically lower the chances of them leaving – mostly due to them being in the place they belong however some team members outgrow the team and want to continue their journey elsewhere.

You may have helped them to become a great leader or a great entrepreneur and now they want to do things for themselves. This is sad because you lose a great team member but great because they are now following your example. By using the great recruitment systems you have in place you will be able to bring the next team member through in a similar mould so all is not lost.

In addition if you understand the goals of each team member and help them to achieve their goals they will never want to leave. Not only will this allow you a greater understanding of your team members but you can use their goals as a reward or incentive instead of a cash bonus. If you have recruited correctly, your team will not be motivated entirely by money. Regular team meetings to help your team plan, review and improve their goals are a good idea to get that insight and to really help your team members get what they want from life.

One of our clients doesn't give her team a cash incentive for reaching a target that they have control over. Instead, if a team member achieves their target within the deadline, she will help that team member achieve or get one step closer to achieving a personal goal. Whether that is taking Friday afternoons off for a month to spend with their children or buying them flights for a dream holiday, the rewards are the fulfilment of their personal goals which is far more motivating than cash.

Management and communication

Management is not the same as leading. Leading is motivating your team, working on strategy and innovating your services and products as well as your business. Managing is making sure your team are supported, being developed in a safe environment and that they are delivering what they need to and when they need to. You will need to be able to do both and know when to use one over the other.

The only direct team connection with leading is inspiring your team with your vision, your culture and bringing out the motivation when it's needed. With managing it's all about the team.

To manage your team as best as possible you and they will need great communication skills. You will need to be able to get your message across succinctly and adapt your communication style to cater to every team member's preferred communication style.

Having short weekly team meetings and regular one to ones can help with this. The one to ones can be for one minute and as simple as asking 'how are you doing with task A as we agreed that you would have it completed in five days'? Or 'do you need any help from me or any other team member'? Or 'are you still on track to finish in five days as we previously agreed'? It is important for your team to know that you have got their back but that this is balanced with them knowing that they must do what is required of them. Create a system for reminding you to check in with team members. Voice memos to an assistant to schedule task reminders or appointments is one system or use your voice command on your mobile phone.

You will need to keep the team informed about what is going on in your business, update them on projects relevant to their role and hold them accountable.

Teach your team to keep to the facts when communicating with you and to value their time as well as yours. When they have an issue or problem it is their responsibility to come up with two possible solutions before asking for your approval to go ahead with the best solution. This means that rather than coming to you with a problem they come to you with a solution that you can say yes or no to without too much work or thought on your part.

On low level pieces of work you can let your team deal with the problems themselves and let you or their manager know what they did after the work was completed. You want to empower your team to make decisions for themselves and create a safe environment so that if they do make a mistake it is easily dealt with and that your business is a hotbed for learning from their mistakes. Trust your team to do what is required of them and do what is right for the business. If mistakes are made they will be able to learn from it and update any systems that need updating.

With delegation there are four levels:
- Wait and don't do anything until told by you,
- Ask for your permission then act,
- Act and get your approval as work is being done,
- Act and let you know about the task once it is complete.

You can choose the most appropriate level of delegation depending on the team member and the task but you will want to gradually move to a higher level where possible. The movement will come from learning from mistakes or learning and support from you or others within your business. Only tasks that could have catastrophic impact on your business should be kept at a lower level of delegation to allow you or another manager to fix things, if required, before it is too late.

As long as the results of their work and the time taken to get the results is good and the team follow the systems then that is fine, it doesn't have to be perfect.

This is what normally happens in business: Let's say you promote a team member to manager for doing good work because she was excellent at her work. Then as a manager she notices that most of the team she's managing are not working to the same level as she once did when she was in their shoes. So the manager gets annoyed and starts doing some of the work instead of her team.

The problem with this is that the manager is no longer managing the team and has more work to do than she should have, the team don't feel trusted to do their work and become reliant on the manager to help and do the work because they know the manager will always help them. As a result the manager becomes overworked, she doesn't produce the result you expect of her and the team get lazy, leading to a poor work environment and your business not necessarily progressing as you would have expected. The manager needs to manage and accept good results are good enough and the team need to be trusted and managed to get the work done when it is required. This knowledge and work environment comes from education, training and practice. You will need to make sure any managers in your business as well as yourself can manage the team well.

When communicating with your team you need to choose the right communication method relative to the content and the urgency of the matter but also consider the preference of the team member. This may mean a quick check is done by a prearranged phone call, a detailed plan is sent by email or delivery of an important task is discussed at a face to face meeting.

When communicating with your team you need to remember three things:

- Empathy – Understand the position of the person communicating with you, stand in their shoes and see it from their perspective, emotions and beliefs.
- Listen – Listen to the facts, the total message and understand what is being explained. Give your full attention to your team member and be silent when they are speaking. Make notes on your thoughts as they speak and even ask their permission to make notes beforehand so they understand what you are doing.
- Good questions – Ask good open ended questions that show you have been listening and to help you understand if it wasn't clear. Your question should encourage more communication.

Teach your team this too when they are communicating with you and each other. If everyone knows and understands what they need to know and the environment is empowering and supportive there will be no stopping them.

Measure performance

The performance of the team should be measured at least on a monthly basis. After the team goal planning session it will be ideal to review with the team how well they have performed for the previous month by comparing their actual performance to their targeted performance.

With your team you will set their targeted performance on areas of the business where each team member has control. Control is important because without it the team member cannot influence the output no matter what they do. This will lead to your business goals not being met and the team member not being motivated because they cannot control whether they hit their target or not.

For example, for your sales team you wouldn't give them a target for the number of leads the business gets in a month. This is a result from your marketing team. Your sales team will not be able to influence the number of leads because they sell to the leads, they don't generate leads. So a target for your sales team could be to have a 50% conversion rate for the month. This way your sales team know they need to get one new customer for every two leads, which is in their control – after all they are supposed to sell!

It is really important that the targets for each team member are aligned with your business goals. So for year two, if you want a customer base of 200, the conversion rate for the sales team and the number of members in the sales team will need to be appropriate to hit that number. You aren't giving the team targets for the sake of it or to boost morale. The targets are to help you achieve your business goals and to reward the team if they help you get there, particularly if it is ahead of schedule.

It is also a good idea to make sure the goals of each team member are still relevant and that they can achieve their goals through their work in your team. As long as this is the case, the team will remain highly motivated.

When comparing each team members actual performance to their target the question you want to ask the team member is 'why'. Why did they exceed their target this month? Why did they miss their target this month? Then their answer will help you and them to answer the following questions. Was the target the right amount? Is the target area the right area? Are the processes in that area of the business working correctly? Does your team member have control over that area?

Once you get to the bottom of why the results occurred as they did you will then either be able to fix an issue or make the most of an opportunity.

You ideally want to arrive at a place in your business where you can say if a result in your business is not as you expect it is the systems and processes that will be wrong, not the people that use them.

To enable you to take this approach you will need to make sure you have recruited the right team members based on their personality and attitude so they fit with your business culture and the rest of the team. The team members will need to have enough of a skill set to follow the procedures, understand the systems mindset and understand why the systems mindset is so important. You will need to provide training to educate the team on the procedures and systems used in your business.

At this point your team will always do the right thing and follow the system but they will also be able to spot problems and innovate to improve the systems they use. The systems in your business will need to change not the people.

To record the goals, target performance and actual performance for each team member you can use a Personal Dashboard (PD). As it sounds, this is a single A4 factsheet that includes the goals of the team member and the key areas and results of that team member. Detailing how the areas are measured, the targets and the actual performance.

It is then easy and quick to see for you and the team member if their performance is in line with your expectations and whether they are working towards their goal.

There is also space on the PD for notes and key actions that need to be taken after reviewing the PD results. This will be the action plan for the team member, and possibly you if you need to be involved with system changes or training, for the month ahead. It will clearly show what improvements or maintenance is necessary to get the required performance.

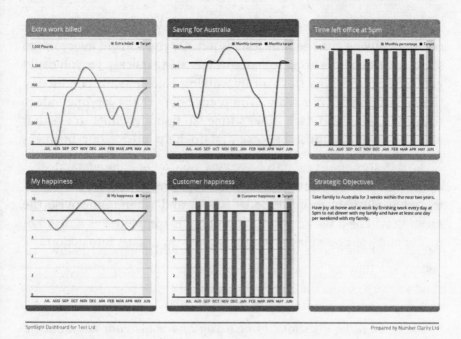

Spotlight Dashboard for Test Ltd

Prepared by Number Clarity Ltd

When creating action plans it is essential to understand who is doing what and by when. So set a deadline and get agreement from your team members that they will do what they need to do by that date. Also, ensure that you will complete any tasks that you need to do by the agreed deadline. If you don't do this then your team will lose their faith in the system. Sometimes you need to lead by example.

One final thing to consider when meeting with your team, is to only meet with them if it is necessary and of benefit to the team. This could be where you need their input or they need to report back to you and the team or a training exercise etc. And only involve the team members that need to be in the meeting. The worst thing you can do with your team is to have meetings that waste time.

There are some topics that will require a meeting but it is up to you to decide when, for how long and what you meet for. Your management team will need to meet with you to discuss what is happening with the business and to help with the strategies you take but this could be weekly, fortnightly, monthly or quarterly. Your team will need to meet at least monthly to review their performance and their goals but you may feel that you can do this on an individual basis.

To help keep meetings on schedule you can have a countdown timer where everyone can see how long is left. Or you can get everyone to stand up instead of sitting to move things along quickly. Or you could get some exercise and fresh air by walking outside while conducting the meeting with your team. The point being that everyone values their own time, and each other's time, so nobody wants to waste it and the meeting must be essential to help push your business forward.

At the end of each meeting always have an agreed action plan detailing what is going to be done by whom and when. Otherwise the meeting will be a waste of time if nothing is completed as a result of it. You and your team must put the topics you discuss into action.

EXERCISE

Here are some questions to help you and your team work out what to measure to track team performance in your business and how to link their goals to your business goals.
- *What are the top ten things about your service/product that are most important to your customers?*
- *Now what are the top three?*
- *How can you measure the top three things and link to the performance of your team?*
- *What are the personal goals of your team members (you'll need to ask them) and how can you link these to your business goals?*

Real world thoughts

Recruiting can seem and often can be a scary process. You are looking for someone to entrust with part of your business, your baby, and want to make the right choice, ideally first time. That's why getting the recruitment process right is really important rather than filling the role. In other words, you don't fill the role until the right person is found.

When I set up the bookkeeping and management reporting business I was scared because this was a new business that didn't exist yet. I didn't know if I could find the right person and get them to stick around for when we did launch the business and then I wasn't 100% sure I could deliver on getting them the work.

Even though I put things in place to reduce the chances of it I still worried about them starting the role and then leaving with all of our clients.

The great part I found for the recruitment process was that it allowed me to practice explaining my vision and why we started the business. If I could get someone to join the team before the business had started I knew I could get my message out to customers too.

My theory was to experiment with various different forms of advertising to find the best place to pick up the right bookkeepers but I was lucky that I found a great bookkeeper in the first place I looked.

I also found lots of bookkeepers that weren't the right fit but they disqualified themselves out of the running because I felt they didn't get my vision and based on their answers to my questions, which included their belief of the bookkeeping industry, their views of the world, view of themselves and their future.

As a team we have weekly hangouts to go through any issues, find what is working well, update the team on the goals of the business and to learn how we can innovate and improve.

I have time available each week for team members to contact me to go through any questions, get an answer to an idea they have for solving a problem or to provide hands on help with something that they cannot do.

My team are great and I always say thank you for their great work and share my gratitude with surprise gifts every now and again. They are brilliant and I want them to know their efforts are appreciated and rewarded.

As this was a new business I asked the team to help me write the processes for the business using the different levels of delegation.

When we first set up the processes and systems for the business it was an overview and created by me. I then asked each team member, with my help, to go through line by line on the process sheets to write down exactly what they do to complete their role. I helped fill in any gaps and to answer questions on the process.

I then got the team to ask me before making updates and now they update the processes and let me know what has been done.

One of the most important measurements for us is the time they feel it takes them to complete their work load. This is important for two reasons; to make sure we have the pricing of our service right because it is a fixed price and to make sure the team are not working at their capacity.

If we had set the price too low we lose money and if the team constantly work to their capacity or above then they will burn out, their level of work will decline and they will quit.

I say we get them to feel rather than record their time because recording your time is a time consuming processes and can often be inaccurate and they will know from a gut feeling if they are working harder than they need to.

CHAPTER SUMMARY

Key points

- Think and act differently, in a way that is fun for you, to attract and recruit new team members.
- Consider the personality, motivation, beliefs and values of the new team member first before looking at their skills.
- Share your business vision to disqualify the people who don't get what you want to achieve or who you are.
- Hire slowly even if that means leaving a role empty for a period of time. It's more important to get the right person than take someone on who will hinder your momentum.
- Share knowledge, develop your team and help them reach their goals while helping you reach yours.
- Management (including the right delegation level) and communication (including empathy, listening and asking great questions) are key for a productive and happy team. It works both ways too.
- Measure the performance and progress of your team on factors that are important to your team and your customers and that your team can control.
- Only meet with your team if it is necessary and create action plans.

Exercise checklist

☐ *Write down how to get the right person for your next role*

☐ *Find how to measure your team's performance and link their goals to your business goals.*

MEASURE WHERE YOUR BUSINESS IS NOW
Understand where you are

If you are not making business decisions based on the current performance of your business then quite simply you are running your business on luck.

You will instead be making business decisions to fight fires or on a gut feeling that you feel will benefit you and your business. If you don't know the hard facts about your business then there is a greater chance that a decision you make will have a detrimental effect on your business.

Your business is the vehicle that will help you get to your dream destination with all of your goals fulfilled. Why would you use luck as a basis to fulfil your dreams? Do you want to fulfil your dreams and do this as soon as possible? Then you will need to start making decisions based on the performance of your business. You will be surprised at how simple the process can be to help you make the right decisions, simply by knowing the hard facts and asking the right questions.

The right questions are those that help you understand and improve the situation. Such questions as:
- Why is that?
- How can we do that in our business?
- What do we need to do to improve this?
- How can we change that?
- Where are we making the most profit?
- Where are we making a loss?

I have seen a lot of businesses in my time and met a lot of business owners and the one thing that is most common is that they do not measure the performance of their business, they don't know their numbers. You may be in the same position so it is essential that you get your numbers to talk to you. Numbers are the language of business and you or someone skilled in numbers needs to interpret them so you can understand what they are telling you. You can then make better decisions and get better results based on the information provided by your numbers.

One business owner I know ran a very successful marketing campaign for one particular service in his business. The problem was his bank account kept reducing and he didn't know why, he had a cash flow issue. It turned out that the service he had marketed and had won a lot of new business for was actually loss making. So every time he completed that service he would lose money, cash would leave his bank account and not come back. He pushed hard for new business with this service which just made the cash in his bank account leave that much quicker.

If he had known the performance of his business and the performance of each service he would have seen that this particular service was losing money and would never have marketed it as he did. He would have first fixed things so it made money and then marketed it or pushed a profit making service instead. That just makes sense doesn't it, it is simple to see that. But it is only simple to see when your numbers are clear enough to enable you to understand them.

The quicker you can get to know where your business is the better as this will allow you to make simple decisions very quickly. You may need to respond to market changes, or you may need to stop a loss making service or you may want to know why one area of your business is so profitable so you can replicate that across your whole business. Getting to know the information as quickly as possible will save you time and money and get you to your goals much quicker. You will be making quick informed decisions based on accurate information instead of wondering what is going on and possibly making the wrong decisions.

So make sure that you get your business performance reported to you each month or each week as quickly as possible. You will use this information to help plot the path to where you want your business to be. From reading the earlier chapters, you will already know where you want to be and now you will know where you are currently. A path can then be easily plotted to your desired future.

There are a number of ways to measure the performance of your business but it is best to start with your endgame plan by checking how your current performance compares to Year one of that plan. This will give you the gap that you need to fill to get to Year one and clarity of what needs to be done to get there. Remember there are twelve months in a year so you have plenty of time to work on filling the gap. Even if the gap seems too big to be filled just remember that each journey is completed a step at a time so that is all you have to do in your business, complete a task that will move you towards your goals each day one step at a time.

People climb Mount Everest all the time, which is a huge feat. They simply do this by putting one foot in front of the other, one step at a time.

Your first business goals will then be created from this gap and you can break this down over the twelve months to give you your monthly or quarterly targets. You now know where you want to be, it is just a question of how. Work with your team or someone outside of your business to help you answer this question and create an action plan to help you achieve your goals.

Management accounts

Management accounts are the most easily available information to see how your business is performing. Management accounts are simply a profit and loss account, detailing the amount of sales and costs you have made for a given period and whether you have made a profit or a loss, and a balance sheet, which simply shows how much money your business has, how much it is owed by customers and how much your business owes to others. It is also essential to review the other reports showing the cash movement for the month, the amounts your customers owe your business, the debtors list, and the amounts your business owes your suppliers, the creditors list, so you know where your cash is being spent, can keep on top of any late payers and make sure you are paying your suppliers to their payment terms.

In a simple nutshell, your profit and loss report shows your business performance for a date range and your balance sheet shows your business position at a specific date.

Reviewing your management accounts on a monthly basis is essential but you will need to know how to read the profit and loss account, balance sheet and other reports. Your bookkeeper or accountant will be able to help explain what your management accounts are saying to you but the tips below will also be helpful.

The first thing you want to do with management accounts is to see if your business is in profit. This is done by checking the profit and loss report and scrolling to the bottom figure, which will show a profit or a loss. A profit means you are making money and a loss means you are losing money.

The next thing you will want to check is that the business has a positive balance sheet value. This is done by checking the balance sheet report and scrolling to the bottom figure, which shows the value of your business. A positive figure means your business has value to a potential buyer and reserves to reinvest or to pay out to you. A negative figure means if things carry on as they are you will not have a business for very long.

After that you will want to check the balance sheet to see the current net cash position of your business. To work this out you will take the total bank and cash amount plus the amount owed to you by your customers and minus the amount you owe to your suppliers, your team and the tax man and any amounts your business has been paid in advance of doing the work. This calculates what your cash position would be if on the date of the balance sheet report all of your customers paid your business and your business paid all of the people it owes.

If the figure is positive then your business has enough cash to function and you want to utilise some of the surplus cash if there are reserves, from the previous balance sheet check, to do so. If the figure is negative then you need to get more cash in to your business, by either making more profit as cost effectively as possible or paying yourself less, because your business will run out of cash. This is pretty simplistic and crude and it purposely ignores borrowings from banks and finance companies as these tend to be long term borrowings.

The point of the calculation is it's a good indication of the current net cash position of your business. Sometimes having a big bank balance can be deceptive, particularly if your business owes large amounts to suppliers or the tax man. So don't just look at your business bank balance to make cash decisions.

Next you want to check if the management reports are as you expected. On the profit and loss report you will want to check that the sales are at the right level and not too low, that each cost heading is not more than you expected and that the profit is as you expected for that period.

On the balance sheet you will want to make sure the bank balance is at the level you expect, the amount your customers owe your business is as low as possible, which indicates that money is in the bank if sales are as you expected, and that your business doesn't owe too much to your suppliers.

If anything is not as you expected, positive or negative, you will need to find out why the figures are different and immediately fix any problems or maximise any opportunity.

You will then want to compare the current month's figures on the profit and loss report and balance sheet to the prior months to make sure you are making progress towards your milestones and to help spot any anomalies. Such anomalies could be higher amounts in one month compared to others or zero amounts in one month compared to other months.

You can then ask the right questions about the performance compared to each month and to your expectations and goals.

For example if your phone costs had tripled this month compared to the previous months you would want to know why, to reduce this cost, right? And if your sales for this month were double for the previous month you would want to know why, to keep the sales this high every month, right?

By reviewing the management accounts it gives you the information to ask the right questions to stop problems as quickly as possible and to make the most of opportunities as quickly as possible.

Also you can compare the performance to the monthly budget to easily see where your business is over or under performing and ask why there are differences between your actual figures and the budget. Your budget is your ideal path to your ideal future. So how is your business performing? Is your business still on the right path or does it need a course correction? That's the true power of setting a budget linked to your endgame when comparing to your current position.

You may then need to update the budget due to under or over performance. How does that affect your plans to get to the figures in Year one? Will you get there quicker than expected or do you need to change something in your business to speed up your progress? What you can do is update the budget to include the total difference from where you are now to where you want to be in Year one and divide that equally over the months that are left until you reach Year one. That way you are spreading any shortfall from the previous months over the remaining months of the year.

Updating the cash flow forecast will also be required to show the new opening balance and to adjust the figures for any additional or unexpected amounts. You may need to move a payment to next month that didn't happen this month etc. Then you can review whether the monthly end balance in the cash flow forecast goes into a negative at any point. If it does you can speak to a lender as soon as possible to help to bridge the gap or you can work on improving cash flow to avoid it. The key is that you know that this will occur in the future so you have time to either stop it from happening or get help to plug the cash gap.

Breakeven Point

As it sounds breakeven point is the point at which your business achieves breakeven. This means the total costs of your business equal the total sales so you haven't made a loss or a profit, you break even.

The reason to know the breakeven point in your business is so you know how much in sales you need to raise in a given period, a year, a month, a week or a day, to ensure that all of the costs in your business are met. You will know exactly how many customers you need each week or what your average sale price per customer needs to be each month to achieve breakeven. As long as the level of profit is in line with what you are expecting in the business you can use this as a more 'scientific gut feel' when reporting on how the business is going.

So for example say you have calculated the breakeven point in your business and it equates to having twenty customers per month. You can then measure how many customers you are dealing with each day within a month, which gives you clarity on how the business is performing in real time.

You may get to day twenty-two in the month and need an extra five customers so you may use your customer and potential customer database to send out an offer to get those five customers.

You may get to day ten and have sold to twenty customers already so you could put your feet up for the rest of the month or do something else instead of working in your business. Or you could continue to sell as every additional customer will create added profit.

This is another reason to know the breakeven point in your business; you will know when the business is making a profit. If you have a profit goal that you want to achieve you will also know how many customers you need to achieve that goal.

The breakeven point is often a surprise because it will either seem a lower point than you imagined, so making good profits seems a simpler task. Or a higher point than you imagined, which will make you pay more attention to the costs you make and the sales you generate in your business.

To calculate your breakeven point you will first need to know your total fixed costs. These are costs that do not change regardless of the amount of sales that your business makes, such as rent, admin team salaries, phone, broadband etc. You should also include any payments that you personally receive from the business through salary, dividends or drawings as these too are fixed costs for your business. This is so often left out but you want to get paid don't you? You can get these figures from your budget if you followed the budget planning earlier in the book. Use the fixed costs for the year rather than a particular month as this will include any seasonality in your business.

You will also need to know your average gross profit percentage. Gross profit is calculated by deducting your variable costs from your sales.

Your gross profit percentage is calculated by dividing your gross profit by the sales and multiplying by 100%. You can use the figures from your budget as long as the budget is as close to the actual performance as possible. Again use the annual figures from your budget.

$$\frac{\text{Gross profit}}{\text{Sales}} = \text{Gross profit percentage}$$

Variable costs are those that are required in order to make a sale. These costs vary depending on the sales that are made in your business such as materials, sales commission, sub contractors, etc.

Now you have the tools to calculate the annual breakeven point in your business. To do so you will divide your total fixed costs by the gross profit percentage.

$$\frac{\text{Total fixed costs}}{\text{Gross profit percentage}} = \text{Breakeven point}$$

Here's an example.

Business A knows from its budget that it has annual fixed costs of £60,000 and a gross profit percentage of 58.5%. So Business A divides the £60,000 by 58.5% as below:

$$\frac{£60,000}{0.585} = £102,564$$

The Breakeven Point (BEP) is £102,564 (rounding to the nearest pound), which means that Business A needs to make sales of £102,564 for the year, or split equally throughout the year, £8,547 per month to break even.

Now here is the fun part.

If the average sale for Business A is £550 per customer, then Business A will need 186.48 customers per year to breakeven.

$$\frac{£102,564}{£550} = 186.48$$

You can't have 0.48 of a customer so we'll say Business A needs 187 customers per year or sixteen customers per month.

So it is clear to Business A that they need sixteen customers per month spending their average amount of £550 per customer to breakeven each month, a total of £8,547 in sales per month. If you do the same process in your business this will link your numbers in your business (sales, costs, profit etc.) to other numbers you may be more comfortable or familiar with (customer numbers, average spend per customer etc.).

You don't have to use customer numbers, this is just one way to represent the breakeven point. You could calculate average amount spent per customer if you know your customer numbers. Or the amount of products or time that you need to sell.

It is also clear to your team as well because they know what the business has to achieve with their help for it to start making a profit. If you have an incentive scheme linked to the amount of profit the business makes then they can clearly see how well they are doing. You will obviously need to regularly share some or all of these numbers with your team so they can see how they are contributing. Essentially the BEP is the minimum the team have to help you achieve. Any extra profit made can be shared amongst everyone in the business.

EXERCISE

- *Using the breakeven example calculate the breakeven point in your business. You will need to know your total fixed costs per year and your gross profit percentage, if you don't have these get them from your accountant.*
- *What is the average sale value and number of customers you need per month to breakeven?*
- *Compare that to what you are doing now, are you out performing or underperforming? What will you do about that?*

Map your sales process

Having your sale process written down and mapped in front of you will help your sales team to learn how the business works and help to systemise your business. But it will also help you understand how the business is currently performing.

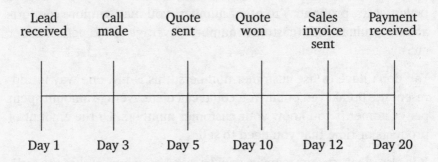

First you will need to draw the sales process in a time line. From when a lead comes in, the first step, to when the cash of a sale is received, the final step. In between you may have a meeting or a phone call (step two), you may then send a quote (step three), you will then win a number of the quotes (step four), a sales invoice will be raised (step five) and the cash from your customer will hit your bank (step six, the final step). For each step write the day next to it. So day one will be the lead being received, the phone call may be day one still or it could be day three, the quote being sent could be day five and so on. From the diagram you can see that the total sales process from lead being received to cash hitting the bank from the customer is twenty days.

You will need to draw out your sales process time line and write the actual days for each step by reviewing what your current time span is in between each step and what is your overall length of time it takes to get paid from a new lead.

What is also really helpful is to include on the time line the number of additional touches that you have with your lead. This could be sending out a brochure as soon as the lead is received, send an email to book the call, maybe even a reminder for the call, send a video or podcast about how your service/product can help after the call, send some customer testimonials after the quote is sent, send a welcome pack once the quote is approved, send an e-book after the sales invoice is sent and then a thank you note when the payment has been made. That's a total of eight additional touches and with the four touches in between the lead received and the payment received that totals twelve touches. These are touches to win the work and to keep your customer delighted.

You may have heard or read that a particular number of touches are required from receiving a lead to making a sale. Depending what you have read and who you have listened to the numbers may be different but the idea is simple. You want to have as many touches as possible in the time frame before a sale – and by the way a sale isn't a sale until the money is in the bank – that are helpful to your prospective customer and that generate additional attraction to your business rather than someone else's. But don't send or do stuff just for the sake of having a touch.

EXERCISE

Draw your current sales process map from when the lead is received all the way through to when the customer pays you for your services/products.

Look for the gaps, count the touches you currently have and write down in a different colour what you can do to improve the process, by making it shorter or by increasing the number of touches or both.

Next, you will need to start filling in some details for each step from the records that you keep. If you are not yet already recording the details then definitely start recording them today. It's best to look over a period of time at least a few months but a year is best.

Keeping to the previous example, here are the details required for each step:

Step One. Leads – The number of leads received over the past year from emails, phone calls, website orders, contact forms etc.

Step Two. Meetings or phone calls – The number of meetings actually attended or phone calls made from your calendar, diary, notes or phone records. Please don't assume that you met with or spoke with all your leads, check your records as you need to be as accurate as possible and you may be surprised that some slip through the cracks.

Step Three. Quotes – The number of quotes sent out from your quote list or quote system. Again take the number from your records and don't assume that all leads were provided with a quote.

Step Four. Wins – The number of quotes that became sales from your quotes and sales invoices records.

Step Five. Sales – The value of each sale for the year and the total sales made for the year from your sales invoice system so you can work out the average sales value.

Step Six. Payment – The date the payment was made, details of any still unpaid invoices and a review to get the details of any bad debts written off.

This information will then allow you to calculate the conversion rates for meeting or call from your leads, the quote sent rate, the quote win rate, the sales invoices raised rate and the payment rate of all sales.

You will want each of the rates to be as high as possible but you will not want the quote win rate to be 100%. If it is your prices are too low, this is an indication that your customer will likely pay you more for your products and services or you haven't included all of the leads for your business.

The final step is to include the cost associated with each step. As we are basing the performance on the previous year, these figures can be taken straight out of the previous year's accounts. So you will include the cost of each lead, the cost of each meeting, the cost of each quote, the cost of each win and the cost of any bad debts. Also the average sale amount will be entered for the sales step 5.

What you will be left with is a cost per activity and the total cost per each step. Total these amounts and then enter all the other costs from your business to calculate your profit for the year which will agree back to the figures in your accounts.

Here are some numbers as an example:

	Quantity	Sale per quantity	Cost per quantity	Total sales	Total costs	Conversion rate
ep one – Leads	1,000	–	35	–	35,000	–
ep two – meeting/call	850	–	20	–	17,000	85%
ep three – Quote sent	800	–	10	–	8,000	94%
ep four – Quotes won	400	–	300	–	120,000	50%
ep five – Sales	400	850	–	340,000	–	100%
ep six – Paid	375	–	850	–	21,250	94%
			Total	340,000	201,250	

mmary

tal sales	340,000
tal activity costs	201,250
oss profit	138,750
her costs	50,000
t profit	88,750

You will be able to see how well the sales process in your business is performing, where the biggest costs are in the process and where there is room for improvement. We'll cover improvement in the next chapter. From following the process you will also understand how long it takes for a lead to turn into a sale. This is key information as it shows that cash after profit is the end result of all the work that happens before. It shows that profit is just a consequence of the processes in your business, it just happens.

So cash and profit aren't going to be a key measure for your business, it will be a key result but not a key measurement. You will instead want to measure the number of leads you receive, the number of meetings attended, the number of quotes sent out, the number of sales converted or the average sale amount. Particularly if your sale process takes twelve months from lead to sale and you have a cash flow gap that needs filling.

Get a template sale process analysis for your business from www.stevenbriginshaw.com/profitsbonus.

Measure your marketing

Your marketing is like anything else in your business, it can be measured but only the key facts should be. Every time you spend money on marketing you should know how much you expect to make in sales in return for the money spent.

Marketing shouldn't be measured because it is a big expense, it should be measured because it can unlock the door to creating accelerated success. Get your marketing right, tweak the right parts and make sure it is profitable and the sky is the limit but you need to make sure your business has the capacity and ability to deliver to the extra customers your marketing will produce.

If your business is like the plumbing system in your home with all of the pipes joined up, no leaks or blockages then your marketing is the tap. You control the turn of the tap as the water drips or runs full blast into the plumbing system, the water represents your new customers.

Test and measure is the mantra for any successful business owner but more so in marketing than any other area. You already know who you are marketing to, what you will say and how you will get their attention from the earlier chapters in the book. Now you need to measure the performance of that marketing.

The questions to ask can simply be:
- How many people saw your advert?
- How many people read your advert?
- How many people followed your call to action in the advert?

- How many people signed up for your offer of a free report, book etc?
- How many of those became official leads in your business?

Knowing these facts will allow you to track the performance of each advert and allow you to calculate how much profit your business is making from each pound spent on marketing. Then if it is making the right amount you just open up the tap a little more.

Here's an example putting some numbers to your marketing for your whole business (there are no sales figures yet as no sales have yet been made):

	Quantity	Sale price	Cost price	Total sales	Total costs	Conversion rate
Adverts seen	5,500	–	2.50	–	13,750	–
Advert call to action completed	3,750	–	4.30	–	16,125	68%
Offer taken from call to action	2,500	–	2.05	–	5,125	67%
Official lead	1,000	–	–	–	–	40%
			Total	–	35,000	

You can now easily see how well each part of your marketing is doing and where there is room for improvement.

Your marketing feeds your sales process with leads and as with your sales process, each part before has an impact on the part that follows. So now let's add the example marketing numbers to the example sales numbers to calculate the profit made from marketing spend, or what is known as return on investment.

THE PROFITS PRINCIPLES

	Quantity	Sale price	Cost price	Total sales	Total costs	Conversion rate
Adverts seen	5,500	–	2.50	–	13,750	–
Advert call to action completed	3,750	–	4.30	–	16,125	68%
Offer taken from call to action	2,500	–	2.05	–	5,125	67%
			Total	–	35,000	
Step one – Leads	1,000	–	35	–	35,000	40%
Step two – meeting/call	850	–	20	–	17,000	85%
Step three – Quote sent	800	–	10	–	8,000	94%
Step four – Quotes won	400	–	300	–	120,000	50%
Step five – Sales	400	850	–	340,000	–	100%
Step six – Paid	375	–	850	–	21,250	94%

Summary

Total sales   340,000

Total activity costs 201,250

Gross profit   138,750

Other costs   50,000

Net profit   88,750

The official leads are the leads in step one of the sales process. You can see that 1,000 leads creates 400 sales. Each lead cost £35 and each sale brought in £850, that's over £24 of sales for each £1 of marketing spend. But you also need to look at profit, not just sales because you could be making loads of sales but no profit. Each £35 lead brings in net profit of £222 (£88,750 divided by 400 sales), that's over £6 of net profit for each £1 spent on marketing. Before turning on the tap to generate more customers you should try to improve the marketing process to make even more with what you already have. Improvement is in the next chapter.

With the example we have looked at the whole business but you should measure separately each marketing channel. Some marketing channels will have more steps than others, but the process is still the same.

And in every marketing channel you can also test and measure how effective your advert headline is, the main content and the call to action by running slightly different adverts at the same time to see which performs best. Then choose the best performing part of your advert and test it again with another slightly different advert at the same time. Keep testing and keep measuring. Only change one thing at a time though as it will be impossible to track what change works best.

To help you track the performance of individual adverts you can use specific webpage URLs and different geographic tracking telephone numbers for each advert. This is helpful for offline and online marketing.

In the same way as any other area of your business you should systemise the marketing so everyone knows what should be happening, when and by whom. And automate as much of the system as possible.

Measure your marketing process with a template from www.stevenbriginshaw.com/profitsbonus.

Business Dashboards

A Business Dashboard (BD) shows the key numbers, financial and non-financial, of your business for the previous month on a single page of A4. These key numbers, also known as key metrics, are those that will make or break your business so by bringing them together all on one page it allows you to make very well informed decisions. The BD allows you to instantly and clearly see how the business is performing in relation to your targets and creates simple decision making on what to do to either improve or maintain the business performance.

You may have seen the film *Ocean's Eleven*, the 2001 remake with George Clooney, Brad Pitt, Andy Garcia, Matt Damon and the rest of the star-studded cast. If you haven't, definitely watch it; it is a good film and you will really get what I am describing below.

In *Ocean's Eleven*, Andy Garcia's character is a casino owner in Las Vegas and each day he is handed a black folder with details of the takings for the day, this is the key number for his business. He opens the folder, looks for a few seconds and then closes the folder shut again. He knows in an instant if the casino is doing as it should, doing really well or doing badly. And this allows him to make instant decisions on what to do next either to maintain things or improve them.

This is what the BD does for your business. Instant clarity leading to instant and simple decision making.

The BD starts with your goals, remember goals need to be **SMART**, and then moves up to what the business needs to be good at to achieve that goal, your core success drivers. Then follows the sale numbers and cost and cash numbers to see how well these areas in your business are doing as they relate directly to the performance of the business. Then the key numbers are reported simply as a measurement to see how well your business is performing in relation to your goal.

Each key number included in the BD has a target number and a way of being measured so you can compare the actual number each month to the target. The targets will be aligned with your yearly vision for the business that you created from the earlier chapter, plotting the path to your desired future.

You will then instantly see if the business is performing as you would like and what simple questions to ask, which will either be 'how do we maintain this performance?' Or 'how do we improve?' You will see the areas that need improving so the next question will be 'how do we do this?' When you have answered these questions it will create your action plan for the month ahead. You and your team will work on these points to make sure that the key numbers on the next BD are hitting your targets.

The BD is a living breathing document. It will be updated at least on a monthly basis, will change with your goals and the key numbers measured may also change. Quite simply it is the most powerful and essential single page in your business.

Here's an example of what a BD could look like for your business. It has the key metrics, which are financial and non-financial, for your business so you can easily see on one page what is going on.

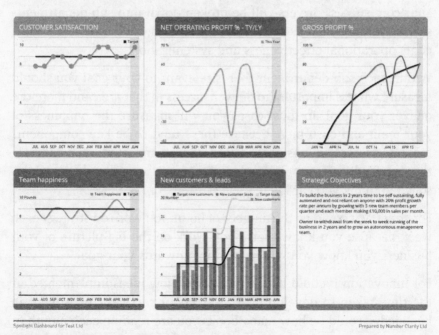

To identify the key metrics for your business dashboard you will need to look within your business to understand what and where the key areas are in your business. It also depends on your goals too because different areas of your business will drive different types of performance. If the goal is for more referrals then you will need to focus on customer happiness and your delivery to those customers. If your goal is for a happier team then you will need to focus on understanding and communicating what will make your team happy and giving it to them. If your goal is profit then you will need to know the key ingredients in your business that will result in more profit being made.

So start with your main business goal and from there work out with the team what areas and functions in your business will be directly related to you achieving your goal. Then you will want to break your business into its functions or departments to see what each department can do to help work towards your goals. These departments are core success drivers – those areas that are essential to get right to create success in relation to your goal – sales and marketing, costs and cash and your key results.

Your core success drivers will be broken down into sub-departments such as strategy, team, customers, innovation, investment in knowledge, operational effectiveness and systemisation.

Within each sub-department that is relevant to your goal you should measure what is important to deliver success in that area and therefore deliver your goal. In most cases you will measure the happiness of your team and customers because these tend to be key components for any success in business. These can be measured for example through feedback, complaints, lost customers/team members and unsolicited thank you cards.

For strategy it could be the number of hours you work on strategy each week because you know that if you work on the big picture of your business you know you will be working towards your goal.

For innovation it could be the number of new ideas implemented or the time taken to develop new products or services. Investment in knowledge could be how many books you are reading each month or the time you are spending on training to develop your knowledge.

For operational effectiveness it could be the percentage of jobs that are completed on time or how much time/materials are wasted each month or on each job. For systemisation it could be how many systems have been written this month or how many systems have been updated.

Once you have found what you need to measure you then need to make sure you can actually measure it simply to give you the information you require. Software and automation are your friend for measuring the key metrics in your business as they will save you time and energy, and there are probably thousands of ways to measure your data. But sometimes a team member may need to do a little data entry or analysis to get the right information.

Finally, you will need to set targets for all the measurements in line with your goal and the goal time line. Then it's a case of getting all of your key metrics together to be reported on your Business Dashboard each month.

EXERCISE

Here are a few questions to help you create your own business dashboard. Some of these questions can be answered from earlier exercises.

- *What are the top three things you can measure about your service/product that are important to your customers?*
- *What are the top three things you can measure about your business that are important to your team?*
- *What are the top three things you can measure about your business that are important to you?*

As well as using your goals as a target and comparing your actual performance to your budget, there are other ways you can compare your business to give you areas to improve and ideas how to do it.

You can compare your current year's performance to the previous five years of your business. This will help you identify what you were good at years ago but are not so good at now or what you are doing well now that you have struggled with before. There may be areas where you have let slip or you have excelled and can replicate in other areas but you may not know this until you actually compare the results. You can even use graphs to help show the performance for the key numbers for your business to get a picture, literally, of how the business has been doing.

You can compare your key numbers to those of your competitors using databases or businesses that will sell you this data. This will tell you what numbers your competitors are able to produce giving you insight into areas of your business that can be improved if you can match their performance that perhaps you didn't think needed improving. The question then is how. Or it will give you comfort knowing that you are outperforming your competitors.

The simplest way to measure your progress and performance though is to compare your actual figures each month to your monthly budget and to measure your key metrics against your targets. This will keep you on track to your desired end destination because you have linked your endgame to your numbers. Where your actual figures and metrics have met or exceeded your targets then you need to maintain the current performance. Where your figures and metrics are less than your targets then you need to improve them. That's simple to see. The hard part is knowing how to improve them. That's next!

Real world thoughts

I love numbers so measuring where my business is now is fun and simple for me. If you don't like numbers or don't understand numbers then I highly recommend you work with someone within your business or a person outside your business who is good with and loves numbers. After all, numbers are the language of business.

Measuring where your business is now is key to understanding what is working well or not so well based on the choices you have previously made and then what choices you will make based on that knowledge.

But I still have had times when I've fallen prey to making choices without the facts of my business performance simply because I chose to spend my time doing something else rather than understand the performance of my business.

Even though I love numbers I sometimes choose not to take the time to understand what is going on. Looking back, I did this because I didn't want to see the results. I already had a gut feel for what was going on and it scared me to see in numbers, the hard facts, what I had feared was true that the business wasn't making the profit it should be. It was failing.

I stuck my head in the sand which is so easy to do when things aren't going the way you want and you just hope things will change. I did eventually pluck up the courage to schedule in the time to review the numbers and then swiftly act at that point to get things back on track.

It is really hard to face your fears, particularly if you have a sense of what is going on but the only way you can get out of the tricky situation that you fear is to face it head on. This is even easier to do if you work with someone else who interprets the numbers for you because there is no hiding place, another reason for working with someone outside of your business to hold you accountable.

If you are going to look at the figures on a profit and loss report, balance sheet or any other report then you should compare these numbers to something else. On their own they are pretty worthless unless you compare the figures to your expectations, your budget, the previous month or previous year. You are then comparing the numbers to other numbers that are relative and can then ask the questions 'why is that different?' or 'what happened there?'.

That's it to understanding numbers. Just compare them to other numbers that are related in some way and ask questions.

I really like the breakeven point calculation to help calculate targets but I don't really use the calculation for much else. It gives a very clear picture of the number of sales that are required over a period of time, each day, week, month etc, so the sales team know exactly what they need to do.

Sometimes though and something to be aware of is the cost figures will change which will impact the breakeven calculation and either increase or reduce the sales target required to breakeven. This will need to be communicated to all of your team so they know the goal posts have moved and rightly so they will want to know why so you will need to explain why costs have increased or decreased.

Mapping your sales process is a great exercise to do simply because it gets everything out of your head and on to paper. This is great to see where there are any gaps or areas for improvement but also to help get your sales process systemised.

From my experience business dashboards are a real favourite for business owners who don't like numbers. The reason is the dashboard is very visual and colourful with charts and graphs. As long as the charts and graphs are understood then the numbers are easy to understand in a vivid image instead of black and white numbers.

Be careful though not to measure something for the sake of measuring it. If the measurement isn't really telling you anything about your business or not giving you insight to move you towards your goals then stop measuring it.

CHAPTER SUMMARY

Key points

- Measuring your business allows you to run your business on purpose by making decisions to get where you want to be based on what the numbers are telling you.
- Your profit and loss report shows you the performance of your business for a specific date range.
- Your balance sheet report shows you the position of your business at a specific date.
- Use your monthly management reports to at the least check your business is on track with where you want it to be.
- Using numbers to make decisions is based on comparing numbers with other numbers that are related and asking questions about why and how they are different.
- Calculating your breakeven point allows you to understand what your business must do in sales to cover all of the business costs, including your dividends or drawings.
- Your sales process map helps you systemise your sales and get a clear picture on the experience your customers receive and how efficient you are at delivering it.
- Measure your sales and marketing process with actual costs and sales figures to see where you can make improvements.
- Your business dashboard will give you a living, breathing and vivid visual of your business. But only measure things that make a difference.

Exercise checklist

Find your breakeven point

Write down your sales process map

Write down what you can include on your business dashboard

Get a sales process analysis template and a measure your marketing template at www.stevenbriginshaw.com/profitsbonus

IMPROVE YOUR NUMBERS
Measurement leads to improvement

You read in the previous chapter the importance of knowing how well your business is performing in a number of key areas and now you will be able to improve the current results of your business. The measuring also helps you identify which areas in your business to improve for the quick wins, the biggest returns, the best fit with your goals or simply to stop a big loss.

Whatever it is you want to improve you will easily be able to see from measuring results of your business and can start working on the question how do we improve this area and put your thoughts into action. Measuring helped to create simple decisions or turned a fuzzy uncertain picture into a clear vivid picture.

There are three main areas that you will be able to improve after measuring your business from the previous chapter. These are profit, cash and time. Below is a summary but each has its own chapter following this chapter.

Profit because you will clearly see how much profit the business is making and what drives your profit because profit is simply a result, it's a consequence of doing the right things in your business. The right things by giving a great customer experience to all of your customers, by having a motivated, happy and productive team, in your sales process, in your marketing, knowing your ideal customers etc. Do things the right way for your customers, your team and for yourself and the profits will just follow. From the measurement of your business you will see where you can make more profit than you previously thought was possible.

Cash because you will clearly see where the cash in your business is being used, and if there are any bottlenecks and for how long, where cash is not in your business bank account. The flow of cash through your business really is the most important thing to keep an eye on.

Without cash you have no business. Turnover is vanity, profit is sanity and cash flow is reality. From the measurement of your business you will see where you can get more cash into your bank accounts and not just from the additional profit.

Time because you will clearly see where you as the business owner should be spending your time and what tasks you shouldn't be doing. Time is very precious as it is finite. You only have one life and you should make the most of your time by doing what you enjoy and what you are passionate about, making the money you deserve and working with great customers and a great team. You get the same twenty-four hours as every other business owner yet some are way more successful than others. The successful business owners know the value of their time and use it wisely to get stuff done, the stuff that only they can do. Everything else is delegated or outsourced. From the measurement of your business you will see where you can better spend your time to get what you want out of life and the improved profit and cash will help pay for the team whom you delegate and outsource.

To whet your appetite, here is an example, with kind permission from AVN, of how simply changing your price can have a positive effect on your profit, your cash and your time.

Imagine that you sell ten packets of tea at £10 each, that's £100 of sales. Each packet costs you £5, that's £50 of variable costs and let's say the fixed costs of your business are £40.

What you will see below is the current profit for ten packets.

Sales £100
Variable costs £50
Fixed costs £40
Profit £10

You may think that given the situation with competition, the economy etc that reducing your prices is a good idea so what would happen if you decreased your prices by 10% and this gave you say 10% more customers. Below is a side by side comparison of how the profit in this situation would look like compared to the profit calculation of selling ten packets at £10 each.

Sales £100	Sales £99
Variable costs £50	Variable costs £55
Fixed costs £40	Fixed costs £40
Profit £10	Profit £4
	10% more customers
	10% lower price

A decrease in price means that your profit reduces from £10 to £4. In fact you will need 25% more customers to just get the same profit as before, so a price decrease isn't a sensible approach.

Now let's say that you increase your prices by 10% but you lose 10% of your customers, those price sensitive customers that you didn't want anyway. Below is the side by side view of the profit calculation.

THE PROFITS PRINCIPLES

Sales £100	Sales £99	Sales £99
Variable costs £50	Variable costs £55	Variable costs £45
Fixed costs £40	Fixed costs £40	Fixed costs £40
Profit £10	Profit £4	Profit £14
	10% more customers	10% less customers
	10% lower price	10% higher price

A 40% increase in profit, 40% more cash available because there are fewer packets to buy and more time for you as you now only need to service nine customers instead of ten. Not a bad result! But there is one more scenario for you to consider.

Imagine that you have educated your customers about the price increase and most of them stay with you and in fact you win a few more customers because they heard about your great services from existing customers. So with the 10% increase in price you also get a 10% increase in customers. Below is the side by side comparison.

Sales £100	Sales £99	Sales £99	Sales £121
Variable costs £50	Variable costs £55	Variable costs £45	Variable costs £55
Fixed costs £40	Fixed costs £40	Fixed costs £40	Fixed costs £40
Profit £10	Profit £4	Profit £14	Profit £26
	10% more customers	10% less customers	10% more customers
	10% lower price	10% higher price	10% higher price

A 160% increase in profit and 160% more cash. This does mean that you will have 10% more customers to service but with the extra profit and cash you can afford to pay to delegate or outsource some of your work so you can still end up working less than you are now.

These are just small numbers to keep things simple but imagine there is an extra three or four noughts at the end of the profit in each column. Is that more like your business? Can you see how knowing your numbers can help to transform your business and your life for the better?

More profit, more cash and more time. That's how powerful getting the right price is on your business, your life and the lives of those close to you.

Not only that you will get rid of those price sensitive customers, the BMWs – Bitchers, Moaners and Whiners – those customers that you don't enjoy working with and suck up most of your time.

EXERCISE

Grab your latest set of annual accounts or most recent monthly management accounts as well as the number of customers you have served in that time frame and use the figures from the profit and loss report to calculate the following:

- *What would happen to your profit if you reduced your price by 10% and gained 10% more customers?*
- *What would happen to your profit if you increased your price by 10% but lost 10% of your customers?*
- *What would happen to your profit if you increased your price by 10% and gained 10% more customers?*

Before you go and increase your prices please don't just increase them and expect your customers to pay. You need to explain to your customers about the price change, you may give plenty of notice for the price increase and explain the value you provide to them that justifies the price they will be paying. You may want to test the new price on a section of your customers to measure the response. If you make the price increase in the right way you will be on your way to fulfilling your dreams.

Annual price increases are something to consider too especially if you are delivering more value to your customers each year through innovations and improvements.

Another price consideration is to understand what pricing method you are currently using. Are you using an hourly or day rate price, a fixed price or a value price?

An hourly or day rate is as it sounds you get paid for the work you complete based on how long it takes you to do so. You or the customer have no idea what the end price will be for a piece of work and there is no incentive for you or your team to create efficiencies to get the job done quicker because you will get paid less, unless you lie on your timesheet.

A fixed price is a price arrived at, most likely, through a calculation of an hourly or day rate multiplied by an estimate of how long it will take. Sometimes the fixed price will include some element of value pricing. This means your customer knows exactly what the price will be for the work and it gives you and your team a budget to get the work done in a set amount of time. Here's where you get rewarded for finding efficiencies and innovations to get the work done quicker.

A value price is based on the perceived value from your customer and has nothing to do with the estimated time it takes to complete or your hourly rate. This is based on how valuable your solution is to your customer's problem and how much they want the solution based on the intensity of pain they are in. This too is a fixed price so it gives peace of mind for your customer and it allows for efficiencies and innovation in your business but it also allows for delighting the customer because you can spend more time dedicated to that customer and you enjoying more profit.

The value price can be a percentage of the value received by your customer or if the value received is not easy to put a figure on it can be a figure that you and they feel is fair based on that value they receive.

A simple example of value pricing is when a customer asks you to complete a job for them immediately because of an imminent deadline they have. The customer will feel a great deal of pain by missing the deadline so you can charge a higher price simply because they value having the work being completed quickly in order to meet the deadline.

Moving to value pricing means you tend to need less customers to get your desired profit so you and your team have more time. This is because value pricing is slightly higher than any other pricing method.

With that extra time you can spend more time focused on delighting your customers instead of just satisfying too many customers than you can really handle. With the extra profit you can hire more people in your team instead of spinning too many plates all at once.

You may be thinking that there is no way you could implement value pricing for your existing customers, which may be true. So leave your existing customers where they are and instead think of a market or niche you can serve where they are in intense pain and would pay a higher price for the solution you offer. There is a market for everyone, you just have to find it.

Here is an example of each method of pricing for my bookkeeping and management reporting business.

Hourly pricing

With hourly pricing the price will simply be an hourly rate, say £25 per hour multiplied by the number of hours it takes to complete the work. Let's say with a particular customer some months it takes twenty hours, others it takes twelve and sometimes it takes fifteen.

The price per month will vary from £500 to £300 based on how much work there is and how efficient the team are at processing it.

Fixed pricing

Let's say we sat down with the customer advised them of all the information we needed, when we needed it by and agreed a cap of hours spent of fifteen hours per month to complete their bookkeeping and prepare their management reports but were also able to include some additional services to better help them understand their management reports. Any other work would be extra but a quote would be sent for approval before that work would be completed so the customer has peace of mind and we are fairly rewarded for our work.

If we used the hourly rate of £25, in this case the monthly price would be £375 plus an extra £150, the value we agreed with the customer to go through the management reports with them, the total price would be £525 before charging for any extras.

Value pricing

Let's say we have a discussion with the customer before they came to work with us and found that they were completing their bookkeeping instead of doing other business owner activities (this customer loves to sell).

From our discussion we work out that they can earn £200 per hour from their time when selling and completing other business owner duties. We also find out that the bookkeeping takes them thirty hours per month and they have no idea how to produce management reports let alone what they mean.

Now we are able to work out that if they didn't complete the book-keeping themselves they could earn an extra £200 per hour multiplied by thirty hours per month, that's additional income of £6,000 per month. Also we can explain to the customer the importance of having management reports and explain what they can do when read and understood. As a result we agree a value of £500 for being about to understand and utilise the information in the management reports to help make better business decisions and therefore make more profit.

Add the £500 to the £6,000 and that's £6,500 per month of value that a bookkeeping and management reporting service can offer to them. Now it's a discussion with the customer to work out how much they are willing to pay to get access to that value that we both feel is fair. At this point it is like asking the question, 'if I gave you this £10 note would you give me £3?'

Let's say it's agreed that 15% is a fair value, which is £975 per month. That is £450 more per month than the fixed price method and £475 to £675 more per month than hourly pricing. That's equivalent to two to three more clients on the other pricing methods.

You may be thinking, 'well my competition will charge less so that customer will just go and work with them'. That is true they may be charging less and if that customer is price sensitive then you don't want to work with them. You want to build relationships with your customers and delight them beyond their expectations so regardless of what they pay you they will be singing your praises to everyone they meet. You only want to work with the people that really get what you are doing and appreciate your solution. They will need a bigger budget than a penny pincher, if the customer actually thought about one to start with, but they will not be concerned by price.

It doesn't matter what everyone else is charging because their service is completed by them, not by you and most likely they are not thinking of delighting the customer like you would do if you were value pricing. You bring unique skills, experience and views to your business and the right market will gladly pay to have access to that to help them solve their problems and move them out of pain.

If you do get price objections this is a good sign. It means the customer is more than likely willing to buy but they just need more information to make the purchase. This is your opportunity to educate your customer on why the price is the price and what they receive at that price. Not just the features and benefits but the solutions to their challenges and the value they receive, which if you have priced with value pricing you can remind them that the price is insignificant to that value.

They may say that, 'Joe Bloggs down the road is cheaper' but the likelihood is what Joe Bloggs or someone else is offering is completely different to what you offer. The most likely reason Joe Bloggs is cheaper is because they offer less value to their customers than you, thus a lower price.

They may also say, 'that's expensive', but again expensive compared to what because what you offer is most likely completely different to what someone else offers. This means it's impossible to compare like for like and therefore your help isn't expensive it's more value and therefore a higher price.

Price is linked to the value received, that is a fair exchange and is the idea to explain to your customers when you get price objections.

If after you educate your prospective customer and they decide not to buy then that is also a good thing. You got the chance to practice your price education piece and you defended yourself from not taking on what would most likely have been a difficult and price sensitive customer.

In my accountancy practice we would often get price objections because what we offered was so different to the prospective customer's previous accountant. In the end I loved the price objections and welcomed them because I knew at this point they wanted to buy but just needed to understand what value they were getting.

EXERCISE

- *What pricing method are you currently using?*
- *What pricing method would you like to use?*
- *How can you use that pricing method for new customers starting from now?*
- *How can you put a figure of value on the solution you offer to your customers?*

- *What questions do you need to ask to ascertain the value you bring to your customers through your solution?*
- *What questions can you ask to understand the level of pain they are in without your solution?*

Accountability from an expert

Being held accountable by someone outside of your business who is an expert in their field is a great way to ensure that the right things are done to improve your business. That can be a mentor, your coach or a colleague who will help you work towards your goals, work on your key numbers or complete a project.

By working with an expert you will access their knowledge, experience and skills that you need to help you and your business get to where you want to be. You will have a great trust in them as they will have in you.

By working with an expert outside of your business there is no influence from internal business politics. Instead only the facts are discussed and worked on which cuts through the day to day fluff.

Stepping out of the day to day of your business to work on strategy, marketing, the numbers and your goals will make sure there are no distractions and you are completely focused on moving your business forward towards your goals. You get the time to think without worrying about an email, a team or customer request. You can talk through an idea, opportunity, problem or solution with someone who will listen. Often you will not need much input because by speaking your thoughts out loud it will help you find the answer to your questions. Having someone who will listen to you and understand you is a comfort that you can use to get clarity. The expert will ask the right questions if they need to intervene which will help find the answers you are looking for. Sometimes they will ask the questions you cannot see or the difficult questions you don't want to ask yourself. They have that objectivity and a different viewpoint that will help you see clearly.

The expert will also be there if you need any help but they won't do tasks for you. Instead they will help you understand what you need to do and why or to find a better way of doing it. You will create an action plan together that is prioritised and includes who in your team will do it and with a deadline.

They will give you a kick up the backside if you need it to get the right things done. If you are not working towards the tasks that you agreed to work on you will not only be wasting your time and money but also their time and money.

Working with an expert will allow you to focus on the things in your business that you enjoy and only you can do. The expert will work on the numbers and explain them to you in plain English. They will be able to quickly and easily read the information, understand and give you great feedback or ask you the right questions. They will know instantly how the business is performing now, understand what the business performance needs to look like to get you to your goals and how to bridge that gap.

The expert can cut through all of the information and quickly get to the key points, the information that you need to know, instead of you having to look for the right information and spend time away from what you love doing.

It is really important to get away from the day to day of the business, get out of your office and into a different environment. It allows you to leave all of the day to day stuff at your office to free your mind to simply think. At the office you are constantly doing something and never get the time to think unless you book an appointment with yourself to do so. Finding a place away from your business will get your thoughts flowing and help you to focus on where you want to be, how you are going to get there and what you need to do. It allows you to get the ideas out of your head and you can see if they will work or what will need to be done to get them to work. It will become clear what you need to work on each day, how to do it and why you are doing it.

You will want to do this at least quarterly to make sure you are on the right track, the right things are getting done and you have time to collect new thoughts about your business. There is no standing still in business, the pace of change is quickening all the time. So you need to ensure that you are constantly moving the business forward otherwise you will be going backward.

We have either quarterly or monthly meetings with our clients to help them understand their numbers, we ask them the right questions and give them time to think and work on their business.

Real world thoughts

I do believe that what you measure will improve by virtue of you measuring it.

Improving your numbers is a natural next step from knowing the numbers in your business so the improvement of what you measure makes sense. It's hard not to want to improve an element of your business once you know about it, especially if what you know is not delighting your customers or getting you to your goals.

But, as previously mentioned, what you measure is really important so measuring the number of cups of coffee drunk per day isn't really going to be helpful to your customers or your goals.

I love the example of the packets of tea in this chapter because in such a simple way it explains how reducing your price is bad and raising your prices while educating your market is much more profitable for everyone.

One of the biggest mistakes I see with businesses, and I know because I made this mistake too, is charging a lower price than their competitors.

Here's how I did it but if you replace me with you it may be your story too.

I started a business on the side of my day job doing bookkeeping and some accounts work for family and friends. I had no idea what to charge for the work so I decided to stick to what I knew from my day job, which was using an hourly rate for the work and arriving at a fixed price for the customer.

I knew how long a job would take based on my own experience but I didn't know what my hourly rate should be so I looked at my hourly charge out rate at my day job. I thought 'there is no way I can charge that!', which is silly really because a market already exists for the service at that price but for some reason I felt my service would be seen to be not as good as an established accountancy practice and because I worked from home my fixed costs were much lower than a 'normal' accountancy practice.

So I looked at my salary hourly rate and thought 'that's not enough' and chose a price in the middle.

This happens all the time. Business owners charge less for their time because for some reason they feel they need to be cheaper than the competition. Possibly like me because they think a new business cannot charge the same as an established business and because their costs are lower they can afford to charge lower prices.

What this means, as I found out, you end up with loads of clients because you are so cheap who demand loads of you, they tend to pay late and the minute they find someone cheaper they will stop working with you.

From this position it is really difficult to increase your prices back to the market rate simply because your customers have been spoilt and they are the wrong type of customers. What you need to do in this situation is understand what your customers really want and place value on and educate them in the value you do provide them and why they should pay more for it.

The way I did it was to understand what help they wanted and the challenges they faced so I could create packages, bronze, silver and gold, to include the stuff they required. The bronze was the baseline service with more and more help included in silver and gold.

This was helpful to get the price increase for two reasons. One, there was no other accountancy practice to compare like for like to my packages because they were unique. Two, the uplift in price from the more ideal customers paid for the lost price sensitive customers. I had slightly more money per month and less work to do, which I invested in getting more ideal customers.

Having people outside of my business, like a mentor or coach, has really helped me too. Not only does it make me follow through with the actions we agreed but it gives me someone to speak to about my ideas, challenges and solutions.

It's like having a sounding board as well as getting help and advice when you need it along with the accountability to keep moving forward no matter what is happening.

I honestly feel I wouldn't be where I am now in my business journey without those experts that have helped me.

CHAPTER SUMMARY

Key points
- What you measure will improve by virtue of you measuring it.
- There are three main areas to improve your business – profit, cash and time.
- Lowering your price tends to be a fast way to failure. Instead increase your prices and educate your customers.
- There are three main pricing methods – hourly or day rate pricing, fixed pricing and value pricing.
- To be able to value price you need to understand what challenges your customers have and how valuable your solution is to them.
- Value pricing allows for the greatest profits and the greatest delighted customer experience because you and your team have more time to focus on your customers.
- Price objections are a request for more information to marry up the value received with the price.
- By working with someone outside your business, like a mentor or coach, they will help you stay on the path to get to where you want to be and if you're lucky be able to fast track some of that journey from their own experience and knowledge.

Exercise checklist
Write down the results of playing with your pricing

Find out more about your ideal pricing method

PROFIT IMPROVEMENT

The best and easiest place to start to improve profit is to complete a profit scenario review. You do this by taking your most recent annual figures and playing with the numbers to see what the profit would look like if things were slightly different. For example you may create three scenarios by changing three numbers in your business by say 2%, 5% and 10%. The numbers you change could be to increase the quantity you sell, increase the average price you sell it for and reduce your costs. You will be amazed at the profit increase from changing three numbers by small amounts.

If you can change...		Scenario 1	Scenario 2	Scenario 3
The quantity you sell by...		2%	5%	10%
The average price you sell it for by...		2%	5%	10%
Cut your costs by...		2%	5%	10%
Your profits will change...	From this year's results of	To	Or	Or even
	£	£	£	£
Sales	575,000	598,230	633,938	695,750
Costs that vary with how much you sell	335,000	334,866	334,163	331,650
Costs that don't vary with how much you sell	190,000	186,200	180,500	171,000
Profit	£50,000	£77,164	£119,275	£193,100
An improvement of...		54%	139%	286%

169

THE PROFITS PRINCIPLES

Above is an example of a profit scenario review, with kind permission from AVN.

The end results are staggering. A 54% increase in profit from scenario one and the likelihood is that scenario two is certainly achievable which gives a 139% increase in profit!

Checkout our website to see how you can complete a profit scenario review for your business and see the increase in profit that you can make from three simple changes. Work out the profit improvement scenarios for your business at www.stevenbriginshaw.com/profitsbonus.

Measuring your business by comparing to the past, your budget, your competitors and what your business could look like will all show you that different results are possible, it can be done. The question is how.

You will probably know that there are three ways to improve the profit in your business. Increase sales, reduce costs or do both. There is actually a fourth way that you may not know and that is using your sales process map from the previous chapter. We'll cover these ways each in turn.

Increase sales

You will already have an idea to do this through increasing your prices, as we just covered in the previous chapter, so below are a few more key ideas to help you increase your sales.

Get your customers to buy more by up selling. Have more than one service option that your customers can choose from with your lowest option being your new increased price. Having three options in a menu format is a great way to help customers choose, and mostly they will choose the middle or top options as long as the additional value in these options are strong enough. The price for the top option should be higher than the middle option and the middle option should have a higher price than the bottom option, with the price difference between the top and middle being a smaller amount than the price difference between the middle and bottom option. Show the top option to your customers first as it may be exactly what they need and will be happy to purchase without seeing the remaining options.

This gives your customers the opportunity to purchase a service that better suits their needs that they wouldn't have previously known about if you just sold your one service option. It will also give you a greater opportunity to make more money from customers that would buy from you anyway.

Get your customers to buy more by cross selling. Let your customers know about your other services at least once a year and have your services on your website, brochure and other marketing information. Listen to your customers and understand their problems and frustrations and create solutions to these to help them.

You may list your top ten customers and think what other services that you provide could benefit these customers. Then give them a call let them know you were thinking about them and make the suggestion of how else you can help them get what they want. At the point of sale is also a great time to inform your customers of the other services you can help them with. Your existing customers are more likely to buy from you again because they already know first-hand what you do, how you do it and the experience they receive. This makes your existing customers much cheaper to win more work compared to the cost of winning new customers that don't know you yet.

Get your customers to buy more often, just one extra sale to your customers per year can make a huge difference to your profit, assuming your service is profitable. By simply asking your customers more often to buy something from you will increase the number of times they buy from you. Make time to speak with your customers and have it as part of your sales system so it gets done every time. Subscription models are great for getting regular sales with your customer as they have subscribed to buy something every week, month or quarter. Or you could launch a loyalty scheme to encourage your customers to buy more and stay longer with a reward for their continued custom.

EXERCISE

Here are a few questions to help you understand the challenges your customers face and the help they need from you.

- *How can you have more regular conversations with your customers?*
- *Would a regular face to face or online get together be helpful to your customers?*
- *With regard to the area of where you can help, what is the biggest challenge your customers face at the moment?*
- *If your customers had a magic wand what would they change about their*   *(fill in the space with the area where you help)?*
- *What are your customers trying to get done?*

Convert more potential customers into customers. If you have completed the sales mapping exercise from the previous chapter you will know what your current conversion rate is. So now you just need to improve it. This is covered in the sales process improvement section in a few pages.

You can also get more customers but you should do this last after the other ideas as this will cost more to implement and you will leave money on the table if you haven't implemented the above ideas and the sales mapping improvements, on the next few pages, into your business already.

Finally, you should never ever give a discount to your customers. Always give your customers something else that they will find valuable but it doesn't cost you much. Below is an example of what will happen to your profit if you give a small discount to your customers.

The dangers of discounts		Scenario 1	Scenario 2	Scenario 3
Sales discount of...		2%	5%	10%
Your profits will change...	From this year's results of	To	Or	Or even
	£	£	£	£
	575,000	563,500	546,250	517,500
	335,000	335,000	335,000	335,000
	190,000	190,000	190,000	190,000
Profit	£50,000	£38,500	£21,250	**-£7,500**
Which is a decrease of...		-23%	-45%	-135%

The results are scary! By giving a 10% discount to your customers you will turn a £50,000 profit into a £7,500 loss, a reduction in profit of 135%. Even at a 2% discount your profit will reduce by 23%. That is a very quick way of going out of business. The thing is your costs remain the same, you don't get a discount from your suppliers when you give a discount to your customers. So reducing your sales through discounts will always reduce your profit but by a scary amount more.

Reduce costs

If you sell less you will reduce your variable costs but if you reduced your sales to zero you wouldn't have any customers and would still have fixed costs to pay. Similarly you can't reduce your costs to zero as this would mean you don't have a business. You can't cut your way to success.

Reducing costs is as simple as paying less for something but it too is about improving efficiency by getting more output for the same or less input.

Improve the working practices and procedures in your business so time is saved on one process so it can be spent on another. Take time out of your day to day tasks to spend time thinking about improving the procedures of one area of your business or one particular task. Get feedback from your team to find out if they all do the task the same way and how long it takes them, try to understand the best practice for that task. Ask your team to report to you in a meeting their top three ideas for improving efficiency in the task that they complete. Your team are your eyes and ears of your business and spend all day in their roles so they will have their own ideas of how they can become more efficient.

Improve the technology you use in your business to speed up and automate as many processes as possible. Technology is always improving at a very fast pace so think about the software, hardware and technology systems you use and review whether there is a more up to date version available that does more than your current version. There will be an initial investment to make for upgrades and improvements but as long as you will quickly get your money back in time saved and over the next year the return on time saved is worthy of the investment then it will be worth doing. You want to free up as much time as possible for yourself and your team so you and they can get more done in the same amount of time.

Train yourself and your team to give yourself and them the knowledge and skills they require to do a great and efficient job. New knowledge and refresher training is a way of investing in your team to make them better for themselves as well as the business. If you improve technology then training is essential to ensure they all understand why the changes are being made and how best to use the new systems. It is essential to educate your team so they know why they are an integral part of an efficient well-oiled machine that is your business.

Sack your rubbish customers. You will have a percentage of your customers, most likely 20%, that take up a lot of your time, most likely 80% of your time and energy, are extremely hard work, your team don't like dealing with them, they pay late and moan about your prices. You need to get rid of these customers to free up your time, make you feel better and give you and your team more energy. How good will you and your team feel each day if all of your customers are a joy to work with? It changes the whole attitude and environment of your business. You can then focus 80% of your time and energy on your top 20% of your customers, those that are a joy to work with and pay on time.

You can grade your customers to help you identify your best and worst customers. Either ask your team or spend the time yourself going through your customer list and answering questions about them. Some of the questions will be general but some of the questions will be on the topics that are important to you and your business.

Here are some general questions:
- Do they fit your ideal client profile?
- Do you like them?
- Do they pay on time?
- Do they treat your team well?
- Do you want to work with them?
- Do they give you quality referrals?
- Do they share the same values as you?
- Do they rarely complain?

Here are some more specific questions that we use in our one to one mentoring business, you will need to work out what customer traits are important to your business to get your specific questions:
- Does the customer implement what they agree to do and on time?
- Do they ask great questions?
- Do they have an attitude towards learning and improving?
- Do we feel they are honest when they answer our questions?

A 'yes' answer is a score of one and a 'no' answer is a score of zero. Once you have the answers to your questions you can add up the 'yes' answers and give the customer a score. So if you have twelve questions you may say a score of eleven and twelve is an A customer, a score of eight to ten is a B customer, a score of five to seven is a C customer and everybody else is a D customer. You can then use this information to work out which customers get access to your time, which customers you will go above and beyond for and which customers you want to stop working with. If a D customer has no chance of becoming a C, you don't need to be subjective here you can ask the customer directly based on your grading questions, then you should sack them.

EXERCISE

- *Write down what questions you can ask about your customers to help you grade them.*
- *You may have noticed the Pareto Principle above, or the 80/20 rule as it is also known by. The 80/20 rule states that 80% of the effect or result comes from 20% of the cause or effort. Here are a few examples:*
- *80% of complaints come from 20% of your customers,*
- *80% of your profits come from 20% of your customers,*
- *80% of your sales come from 20% of your sales team,*
- *80% of your problems come from 20% of your team.*

Once you have identified the 80/20 rule in your business you can then make a deliberate decision to focus your time and energy on the 20% that gives you the most reward and not the most pain.

Reducing the price you pay to your suppliers is simple in theory but needs extra thought for you to implement. You can ask your suppliers for a discount or rebate to create a win/win scenario where possible. For example if you have the cash flow available you can offer to pay in fourteen days instead of thirty days for a 5% early payment discount. Your supplier gets cash in earlier, which is probably their number one priority and you get a lower cost leading to more profit and more cash. If your customers pay you up front before starting any work you will be in a great position to implement this win/win situation. You may want to check your previous twelve month spend with your suppliers to give you some leverage in the price conversation. If you spend a lot with your suppliers compared to their other customers then your suppliers will prefer to keep you spending that amount and not paying someone else instead.

Or you may ask your supplier for more value rather than a discount so you get more at the same price. This way your supplier keeps their income the same, you know how damaging discounts can be, and gives you something extra at a low cost to them, win/win.

You may also want to consider other suppliers in the market to find a cheaper price but you have to ensure that you are getting exactly what you want from the cheaper suppliers, the right end result, the right quality, the right customer experience etc. As in life, you tend to get what you pay for so be careful when finding a cheaper alternative supplier.

One of your suppliers may be a bank or other lender so you may want to renegotiate interest rates and your borrowings to get a better deal and to reduce costs now. I know a business that recently looked around for a better invoice finance deal, found one and went back to their current provider to say they were leaving. The current provider then matched the better deal. The business reduced their costs significantly and saved the hassle of telling all their customers they had a new bank account. And the lender kept their business, win/win.

Increase your sales and reduce your costs

You are limited to how much you can reduce your costs by, but there is no limit on how much you can increase your sales by, so it is always better to focus more of your attention on increasing sales; but keeping costs down is a prudent thing to do as well. So do both by following the ideas above just be aware of what you do first and how much time you spend. Prioritise what action you take first based on the biggest result you will get with the lowest amount of effort.

Sales process improvements

You will have created your sales process map from the earlier chapter so now you can use this to dramatically improve the profits in your business.

Below is the example from the earlier chapter. Now imagine that it were possible to increase each of the steps conversion rates by 5% but the leads stay the same.

THE PROFITS PRINCIPLES

Before

	Quantity	Sale price	Cost price	Total sales	Total costs	Conversion rate
Step one – Leads	1,000	–	35	–	35,000	–
Step two – meeting/call	850	–	20	–	17,000	85%
Step three – Quote sent	800	–	10	–	8,000	94%
Step four – Quotes won	400	–	300	–	120,000	50%
Step five – Sales	400	850	–	340,000	–	100%
Step six – Paid	375	–	850	–	21,250	94%
			Total	340,000	201,250	

Summary

Total sales	340,000
Total activity costs	201,000
Gross profit	138,750
Other costs	50,000
Net profit	88,750

After 5% increase

	Quantity	Sale price	Cost price	Total sales	Total costs	Conversion rate
Step one – Leads	1,000	–	35	–	35,000	–
Step two – meeting/call	893	–	20	–	17,860	89%
Step three – Quote sent	881	–	10	–	8,810	99%
Step four – Quotes won	463	–	300	–	138,900	53%
Step five – Sales	463	850	–	393,550	–	100%
Step six – Paid	457	–	850	–	5,100	99%
			Total	393,550	205,670	

Summary

Total sales	393,550
Total activity costs	205,670
Gross profit	187,880
Other costs	50,000
Net profit	137,880

Wow! What a massive increase those small improvements had on the profit of the business, an additional net profit of £49,130. That's a 55% increase in net profit by having better systems and being more organised. The reason the increase is so large is the improvements from each step also work on each other. This is called synergy or 2+2 = 5, where the result equals more than the sum of its parts.

You may be able to improve those steps in your business by more or less than 5% but the key to the massive increase is to make small changes in a lot of areas rather than make a big change in one area. This is before you get any more leads. You get the extra leads last after making the improvements to each of the steps otherwise you will have an inefficient process and lose out on the extra cash available.

You will also want to review your sales process itself for any additional touches that you can add to the process that will be informative or a 'wow' moment for your prospective customer, something to show that you care about them and not just about the sale.

To see some examples of what you can do to improve the sales process in your business let's take each of the steps in turn, starting with step two, to give suggestions of what you can do to get an improvement.

Step two. Test different ways of asking for a meeting or call. Test the ways of booking a call or meeting. Test having a call instead of a meeting and vice versa. Test different scripts used during the call or meeting. Test using slides at a meeting.

Step three. Have a well written system for sending out quotes. Get the quotes drafted as soon as the meeting/call ends. Ensure all the team understand the system and why the system is there so 100% quotes get sent out. Report on this statistic in team meetings.

Step four. Test different quote wording. Test different methods of sending out the quotes. Test different calls to action to accept the quote. Test a time limited offer to entice a quick acceptance of the quote. Test the follow up process. Test different follow up scripts.

Step five. In the example the assumption is that you will send out invoices for 100% of work you have won. If in doubt, you can send the sales invoice out as soon as the quote is accepted or as soon as the work is completed. Build this into the procedures of your business so you can have 100% certainty that 100% of sales invoices will be raised when they need to be.

Step six. If you operate a sales invoices and payment first policy before commencing any work then you can be sure to avoid any bad debts and non payment of invoices. This will save time and energy chasing the money after the work has been completed.

Test to see if you get any objections for payment in advance from customers after the quotes won step. If you do and really want to work with the customer then consider if you want to allow them to have a sales invoice raised once the work is completed but that it must be paid by direct debit and set up the direct debit mandate there and then. Learn from this if it doesn't work out.

Test different debt chasing processes and better debt chasing scripts to get the money in from the bad payers.

Step one, getting leads, comes last because you need your sales process to be free of bugs and leaks so you don't waste any leads. The first thing you will want to do before increasing your spend on marketing or looking at new media or new channels is to improve your marketing process.

Using the earlier marketing process example this is what would happen if you could improve each of the steps by 5%.

Before

	Quantity	Sale price	Cost price	Total sales	Total costs	Conversion rate
Adverts seen	5,500	–	2.50	–	13,750	–
Advert call to action completed	3,750	–	4.30	–	16,125	68%
Offer taken from call to action	2,500	–	2.05	–	5,125	67%
Official lead	1,000	–	–	–	–	40%
			Total	–	35,000	

After

	Quantity	Sale price	Cost price	Total sales	Total costs	Conversion rate
Adverts seen	5,500	–	2.50	–	13,750	–
Advert call to action completed	3,933	–	4.30	–	16,912	72%
Offer taken from call to action	2,753	–	2.05	–	5,644	70%
Official lead	1,156	–	–	–	–	42%
			Total	–	36,306	

By making those small 5% improvements you would get an additional 156 leads without having to get any more people to see your adverts. Those extra leads have dropped your cost per lead from £35 to £31.40. Now let's see what this does to your profit while working on the 5% improvements of the sales process.

Before

	Quantity	Sale price	Cost price	Total sales	Total costs	Conversion rate
Adverts seen	5,500	–	2.50	–	13,750	–
Advert call to action completed	3,750	–	4.30	–	16,125	68%
Offer taken from call to action	2,500	–	2.05	–	5,125	67%
Official lead	1,000	–	–	–	–	40%
			Total	–	35,000	

	Quantity	Sale price	Cost price	Total sales	Total costs	Conversion rate
Step one – Leads	1,000	–	35	–	35,000	–
Step two – meeting/call	850	–	20	–	17,000	85%
Step three – Quote sent	800	–	10	–	8,000	94%
Step four – Quotes won	400	–	300	–	120,000	50%
Step five – Sales	400	850	–	340,000	–	100%
Step six – Paid	375	–	850	–	21,250	94%
			Total	340,000	201,250	

Summary

Total sales	340,000
Total activity costs	201,250
Gross profit	138,750
Other costs	50,000
Net profit	88,750
Profit per sale	222

After

	Quantity	Sale price	Cost price	Total sales	Total costs	Conversion rate
Adverts seen	5,500	–	2.50	–	13,750	–
Advert call to action completed	3,933	–	4.30	–	16,912	72%
Offer taken from call to action	2,753	–	2.05	–	5,644	70%
Official lead	1,156	–	–	–	–	42%

	Quantity	Sale price	Cost price	Total sales	Total costs	Conversion rate
Step one – Leads	1,156	–	31	–	36,306	–
Step two – meeting/call	1,032	–	20	–	20,640	89%
Step three – Quote sent	1,018	–	10	–	10,180	99%
Step four – Quotes won	535	–	300	–	160,500	53%
Step five – Sales	535	850	–	454,750	–	100%
Step six – Paid	528	–	850	–	5,950	99%
			Total	454,750	233,576	

Summary

Total sales	454,750
Total activity costs	233,576
Gross profit	221,174
Other costs	50,000
Net profit	171,174
Profit per sale	320

Your net profit has increased to £171,174, that's an increase of £82,424 and 93% from the before scenario! And £33,294 of the increase relates to the improvements in the marketing process. You will notice also that the profit per sale has increased to £320 from £222 making your net profit return on marketing spend to be over £10 per £1 spent on marketing. That seems an even more compelling investment than the £6 profit return from the before scenario.

This shows the importance that you first work on your sales process and then you must work on your marketing process to dramatically increase your net profits. You haven't even worked on new ways to get more people to see your adverts yet.

When you are ready to get more leads after improving the sales process and marketing process steps in your business then make sure that you have worked out your ideal customers from the earlier chapters. Once you know who you want to work with you can focus on the message you want them to see that will make your ideal customers want to work with you. Then use the correct media (magazine adverts, online ads, social media etc) to get the message to them.

Also review how many marketing channels you have in your business and which channels you are measuring. Each stream should be measured to see how many leads it produces, how many of these leads turn to customers, how much each customer costs to acquire and what the return on investment is. Then ask yourself how many leads you need to bring in and do you have enough marketing streams. What else can you do to generate leads? Can you use new methods of media? If your marketing is working in one media can it work in a similar media? Can you create a new niche? Get your team or an outsider involved to help you brainstorm some ideas.

EXERCISE

- *What tweaks or improvements can you make to improve each area of your sales process?*
- *What tweaks or improvements can you make one at a time to improve each area of your marketing process?*

Real world thoughts

The profit scenario review is really mind blowing for some people to be able to see their business in a completely different light by making lots of little tweaks and improvements. The profit scenario review gives hope and reignites the flame of motivation because it makes a dream profit figure seem attainable.

It also gets you thinking about how you can achieve those different scenarios, it's a great workout for your mind!

Maybe you take one increase from each scenario rather than a complete scenario but the point is you are moving in the right direction towards your ideal business.

I've found the best way to sell more is to regularly speak and listen to your customers. This not only creates a better relationship but by asking questions about what is going on, what are their challenges and what do they need help with, and listening to the response allows you to create services and products that will actually be helpful to your customers and effectively sell themselves because what you are selling is exactly what they want.

I also found this strange in my accountancy practice that the more we spoke with our customers the more extra work we would get. Not by selling but by asking questions, listening, giving some general advice and then asking if they would like some help with that.

It got to a point where we were running out of available time to service the extra work and had to drop other non-customer tasks to fit the work in. It's a nice problem to have but a problem nonetheless. Looking back, I would have outsourced or delegated more work to free up the space but back then you are simply caught in the moment and can't always see the wood for the trees.

Selling is often feared or disliked by people but I love it. While I was still at sixth form working on my A-Levels I had a part time job at House of Fraser in Reading selling fridges, washing machines, tumble dryers etc. We called these white goods because they tended to be white. I also helped occasionally on the brown goods department, this was TVs, DVD players, Hi-fis etc.

I say I sold white goods what actually happened was they sold themselves. I simply spoke with the browsing customers, listened, asked questions about what they wanted and the problems they have, listened some more and then gave them some advice and a couple of choices based on what they told me.

Very quickly the commission I earned each month was at least 100% more than my basic salary, in other words I at least doubled my salary through my selling.

I must admit the extra money was a driver for me back then so I could buy fashionable clothes, go out nearly every night of the week and have a big blow out every Friday and Saturday night. But the other driver was to help the people that came into my department to find a solution to their problem and give them the information they need to make a decision. That's what I would want so that's what I did for others.

Earning so well nearly stopped me from starting my accountancy and business journey. The salary I was offered as a full time junior trainee accountant was much lower than my part time basic salary at House of Fraser. When adding in the commission I was taking more than a 50% pay cut to get into accountancy.

I had endless discussions with my parents about this and in the end I saw sense that short term loss of income would make up for it in the long run because I was pursuing my, at the time, dream career. Without this decision I wouldn't be where I am today.

There are always ways to reduce cost not necessarily by being a skinflint but by being sensible about where the money goes. If you share your figures with your team they will soon keep you in check because if they have a bonus linked to the net profit of your business they will be watching the fixed costs like a hawk.

It's always sensible to every now and then look at alternate suppliers to check the quality of their service or product and the price compared to what you are getting now. Also do bear in mind the relationship you have with your existing suppliers. If your suppliers have a relationship with you that you are happy with then a change to another supplier will be unlikely to be useful but if you have a non-existent relationship with your supplier then the market is yours for the choosing.

Getting the team involved with helping to find efficiencies and innovations to reduce your variable costs is definitely a smart move because they work day in day out on the processes and can see where improvements can be made.

I remember the first time I graded my customers, the grading gave me a picture of what I already felt was the case but there were also a couple of surprises.

The way I sacked most of my customers was to price them out so they made the decision to leave on their own without me having to push them out. This was a win/win situation because I either got paid the rate I felt I deserved for these lower grade customers or I got rid of them freeing up my time. It was win/win for the customer too, because they got to continue to work with me or they could choose someone else based on price.

Once I built up my confidence I was able to push customers out of the door regardless of how much more they were willing to pay. I realised that once a low grade customer, always a low grade customer and the extra money doesn't cover the mental and emotional energy required to work with them. I should have done this from the beginning.

Like with the profit scenario review the sales process improvements are mind blowing! Tiny increases in each area make a huge difference.

The effect on my accountancy practice was life changing. I focused most of my attention on the sales meeting but also worked on quoting, the price and how I was paid. I wanted to get to the bottom as quickly as possible of the challenges and the solutions required by the prospective customers. I could then really understand their needs and demonstrate my ability to help them. I knew that if I could wow them in that meeting it would mean the price discussion would be far smoother.

At times though I did enjoy price objections. It gave me a chance to practice my ability to educate the prospective customers because price objections are just requests for more information so they can understand why the price is what it is and what they are getting for it.

CHAPTER SUMMARY

Key points

- The profit scenario review will stimulate ideas to improve your profit.
- Increase your sales by getting your customers to buy more of what they want from you.
- Speak with and listen to your customers to find out what challenges they face and what help they want so you can give them what they want.
- Never give a discount. Always give more value.
- Get help from your team to find efficiencies and innovations to reduce costs.
- Free up time and costs by sacking your worst customers.
- Focus your time and energy on the 20% in your business that gives you the most reward rather than the other 80%.
- Use available cash to get a discount by paying early.
- Improve each area of your sales process by a small amount at the same time to have a huge increase on your net profit.
- Get more leads after you have improved your sales process to reduce wasting leads.
- Test and measure improvements one at a time on your marketing to see what gives you better results.

Exercise checklist

Get your profit scenario review template at www.stevenbriginshaw.com/profitsbonus

Write down what questions you can ask your customers to find out what else they want from you

Write down your grading questions and grade your customers

Write down what tweaks you can make one at a time to your marketing to get a better result.

CASH IMPROVEMENT

You will see three main reasons why there is a cash flow problem in your business and it can be one or a combination.

1. Your customers do not pay you on time so you find it hard to pay your suppliers, yourself and your team on time.

2. You pay yourself more money than the business can afford. Have you left enough money in the business for the business tax, vat and day to day running of the business? Your budget will help you answer this question and if the true profit budget for each month is negative after taking into account the business tax and your income then you are currently taking too much money out of the business for the current level of profit. Ideally you should have a separate bank account each for the tax and vat of your business so it can be paid on time when it is due and so you can clearly see what funds are available in the business bank account.

3. Your business isn't making a profit, instead it is losing money. Making a loss isn't just a negative figure on a piece of paper, it is money that physically leaves your bank account, permanently. You need to be aware of any losses as soon as possible to give you the opportunity to turn things around quickly.

When you improve your profit you will improve your cash balance eventually but it will depend on how long your process is from winning the work through to getting paid by your customers. You already have some ideas on how to improve your profit so below are a few ideas and practical points to help you improve your cash flow.

Also, a business requires cash to grow so make sure you use your cash flow forecast to check the cash is flowing in the right direction in your business.

How to get paid quicker

Getting your customers to pay on time is difficult but the first thing you should know is that you have a choice to work with your customers or not. You also have a choice whether to set your payment terms as upfront, after a specific number of days, upon completion or a mixture. You have a choice whether to accept the payment terms your 'big' customers dictate, whether that is thirty, sixty, ninety or 120 days. So ultimately if your customers take longer to pay you than you expected, or if you agree to long payment terms, it is your responsibility. If you have a cash black hole due to the length of time your customers take to pay, it is your responsibility. You are responsible for the choices you make in your business.

So you may find it is no surprise that sacking your existing customers and replacing them with better paying customers, those that fit your ideal customer profile, will actually help you get more cash in your bank account. And make life better for you and your team.

Like most things in life the carrot is more of an incentive than the stick but you have a choice to give more to get paid earlier or to take away for getting paid late.

Below are some ideas that you can implement to ensure that you get paid in full and get paid early.

Improve your credit control procedures so you only give credit to customers that are credit worthy. Review the credit score of your customers before they purchase again. Stick to credit limits by refusing to complete additional work before a payment is made.

Improve your debt chasing procedures. Send out a statement before the invoice is due to act as a reminder. Then have a set procedure for when contact is made by phone, email and post and what will be included in each correspondence to make sure you give your customer every opportunity to make a payment. You will find that the business that shouts the loudest and for the longest gets paid before any others.

Get paid in stages and don't complete the next stage until the previous stage has been paid.

Get paid up front before each stage or entirely at the start of the work. If you are an expert in your industry or offer a specialist service then your customers will be happy to pay up front to get access to you.

Offer incentives to get paid earlier but don't use discounts. Instead use a prize draw that is of interest to your customers or create an early payment club which entitles your customers to additional benefits and value for paying early.

Legally you can charge interest for each day late the payment is made but often these are never paid, it is just used to get payment in. You can also pursue the debt through the Small Claims Court or instruct solicitors to chase the debt or sell the debt to a debt collection agency. These are really a last resort as you may want to work with your late paying customer again and even if you don't the carrot is much better than the stick.

Other ideas to get paid quicker are:

Have a monthly prize draw with a valuable prize but relative low cost to you. Every customer that pays before your standard terms will be entered into the prize draw. The prize could be an extra service or a meal at the best restaurant in town. As long as the prize draw brings in more cash than it costs to supply the prize then it is a winner.

Increase your prices. You can let all of your customers know that you are increasing prices by one ninth but for every customer that pays early, say fourteen days instead of thirty, will get a 10% discount. For example if your price was £100 a one ninth increase, which is 11.11%, equals a price of £111.11. A 10% early payment discount is £11.11, brings the price down to £100. So if you get paid after fourteen days you get £111.11 and if you get paid early you get £100. A great incentive for your customers to pay early and at no cost to your business as the same price is received with the early payment discount, only you receive it earlier.

Offer extra benefits to early payers. You can give exclusive benefits to your early payers such as priority to getting back to them, a special hot line to call, upgrades to more valuable services, access to a membership group or advanced notice of new services.

Create an early payment club. This is one step on from the benefits where you bundle all of the benefits together and give an identity to those that pay early. They will automatically qualify as a member of the club when paying early. They too will automatically lose their membership if they pay on a later date.

Offer finance to customers. When you make an expensive purchase such as a car or a big piece of equipment you will tend to pay for it on a finance agreement. You can offer the same to your customers when they buy from you. There are plenty of finance providers available who will help you offer this to your customers. You get paid once the agreements are signed, the customer can pay in monthly instalments and the finance provider may share some of the profit with you.

For all of the above suggestions it is best to take time out to think what you can offer your customers and what they will see as valuable to make them pay early.

Make sure they are included in your terms and conditions along with any benefits for paying early and any consequences for late payment. Get your customers to sign them and keep a copy on file. You can also remind your customers of the payment terms in the signed terms and conditions if they are paying late.

Pay slower but on time

Make sure that you are using the full allocation of payment terms that you have with your suppliers. If you have thirty days don't pay on twenty-five, pay on thirty. A small number of days will make a big difference to your cash flow. Do make sure that you pay on time though, no one likes a late payer.

Renegotiate payment terms with your suppliers. Ask if you can pay in instalments instead of a lump sum to help with cash flow. Give your reasons to your suppliers to ease their mind as they may be worried that you will not be able to pay them in full.

Search the market for alternative suppliers that can provide the same or better service at the right price. You may be working with the right people already so this will give you peace of mind that they are the right people to be working with.

Try to create win/win agreements with your suppliers to help with cash flow rather than just asking for a discount. For example you may be using a serviced office to forward your mail and occasionally meeting with customers etc. If you explain to your serviced office provider that the bigger your business grows the more space you will require on a more regular basis so you will spend more money with them. Then ask them if they are willing to help you fund the growth of your business so that you can spend the bigger money with them quicker by offering you a contribution towards your marketing by way of a discount over the next six months.

Where you use a supplier regularly and are spending more with them as the business grows you can also ask the supplier to set up a rebate scheme where if you spend a certain amount of money they will give you back a percentage of your total spend. The more that you spend the bigger the percentage.

One thing you can do when your business does have the cash required is to call your suppliers to ask what discount they will give you for paying early. So instead of paying in thirty days you ask what discount they will give you for paying in seven days or upon delivery of their services. Your suppliers will most likely be keen to get the cash in quicker so will be happy to pay for it by way of a discount. This creates a double win for your business because the discount creates more profit which means more cash.

Funding growth

At some point you will have plans for growing the business but will not have the cash available to do so. At this point you will want funding from someone outside of the business.

The best place to start is your bank as you have an existing relationship and hopefully they are in regular contact with you so they will know that funding may be a requirement. Ask for a loan or renegotiations on existing loans in plenty of time before you need the money and give your bank manager all of the information they need to make a decision. Be aware that the bank will most likely want some form of security and you need to be able to demonstrate that you can clearly afford the repayments.

Use invoice finance, which is invoice discounting or invoice factoring, to fund growth, a new project or a cash black hole particularly where your customer payment terms are over a long period. The funding is secured on the amounts due to you by your customers. Invoice discounting is where your business will get a facility to borrow up to 90% of the sales invoices when they are raised with the 10% balance made available when the customer pays. Invoice factoring is the same as discounting but in addition the finance provider will collect the money owed from your customer for you. Invoice finance is great at plugging a cash shortfall but it gets expensive. You may want to repay the facility when the cash from your expected growth comes in. Or you can keep the facility longer but this does tend to be an expensive way to get funding if left in place for the long term.

Ask friends and family to support your business but have a legal agreement drawn up detailing the repayments and what should happen if repayments are missed. Money can be a tricky issue among family and friends so if the loan terms are agreed when everyone is on speaking terms it will help if things should go wrong with the relationship later on.

Get an investor to buy a stake in your business to help it grow by using their expertise and you can use the money received to lend to the business. Or the investor may lend cash to the business. Just be aware that the investor will always want to sell their stake at some point so they need a clear exit plan. You will need to know their plan and who they are expecting to sell their stake to. Be prepared for when they do exit to make sure there is no cash flow or operational problems in the business and know whether the whole business or just their share is to be sold.

The above ideas also apply to funding a cash black hole. As with funding growth you should give your lender all the information they need to make an informed decision and plenty of time before you need the cash. If you can explain why the hole was created and demonstrate why it won't happen again it will help your chances of getting the funds you require. Particularly if cash will return in the near future.

Tax, grants and subsidies

Always make sure you are never paying more tax than you have to pay. You will need to speak to your accountant regularly to ensure this happens so start building that relationship now if you haven't got it already. A good accountant will help you pay the least amount of tax legally possible and will be aware of your viewpoint on tax whether that is to save as much as possible or to help contribute to the tax system as much as possible.

When tax refunds are likely to be due make sure these are claimed as early as possible. This may mean that your accountant will need to complete the year-end accounts and tax work earlier but it will ensure the refund hits your bank account as soon as possible.

Be aware of what grants and subsidies are available in your area by checking with your local authority. You will find funding is available for business growth, training for you and your team and employing young people in your business. The funding may partially or fully cover your cost so it is worth looking into.

Practical points

Complete and send out sales invoices on the same date as the work is completed. This will speed up the date of payment from the customer. Getting paid five or ten days earlier could make all the difference between having money in the bank or not. Or invoice in advance of the work being completed.

Complete a cash flow forecast, showing when cash comes in and goes out, as it will in the worst case let you know when the business will run out of money and when it will have money in the bank again. It will give you an opportunity to stop or fund any future cash flow problems and take advantage of any expected surplus cash.

Pay suppliers over a period of time where possible and where the additional cost or interest charge is not huge. You will pay eventually but it gives you time to find the extra cash needed to make the payments and the cost in doing so is worth it.

Budget with true profit in mind; the profit in the business after tax and after your income is paid from the business. If the true profit becomes a loss at any point you can then do something about it to either improve profit or reduce what you are paid.

Ensure your customers are aware of your payment terms and encourage them to pay early with extra benefits they will value. If your customers do pay late then make sure you have a debt collection process with emails, letters and phone call scripts to get the money in. Remind your customers regularly of your overdue invoice. Those who shout loads for longest tend to get paid.

Create a budget for your personal expenditure in the same way as you will for the business and compare actual to budget to make sure you are not spending more than you thought. This will give you an idea of where you are spending money and where you can save money meaning that you can possibly take less from the business if you don't need as much cash.

Get paid upfront by your customers. This means you don't need to worry about chasing money from your customers instead you can concentrate on giving the best possible service to them. Having cash in the bank is a huge benefit because you will see clearly where and when you can spend.

Measure regularly your actual figures against your budgets and cash flow forecasts, for the business and you personally, to make sure you are receiving and spending cash in the right places and for the right amounts. If not you have an opportunity to fix things or take advantage of improvements quickly.

Credit check your new customers if you are not asking for payment in advance. This will help you understand if they already have cash flow problems and may not be able to pay you when the invoice is due. If they are a high risk then ask for payment upfront, if they decline and don't make a sale with you then the likelihood is you haven't lost a sale but saved yourself a lot of pain because they most likely would have not paid you on time and been a difficult client. Credit check your existing customers twice a year as well because their situation will change over your relationship and change credit terms where you need to based on their credit profile.

Ask your suppliers if you can pay on later terms, say sixty days instead of thirty days. If you give a good enough reason they will often accommodate you especially if it is for a short period of time to help you get off a cash flow bump.

Get paid by direct debit. This allows you to legally take the money from your customer's bank account when it is due, which will limit the chance of a late payment. Direct debits can be used for one off payments but as you will be selling more to your customers this is even more powerful for regular payments. Direct debits are more accessible and cheaper than they used to be.

If you are struggling to pay suppliers then keep them in the loop. Let them know when you will be able to pay them based on your cash flow forecast. Your suppliers will greatly appreciate the information and will likely be more accommodating than if they didn't know.

Keep in touch with your bank manager and send to them your budget, cash flow forecasts and monthly management accounts. They will love to see how your business is doing and if they have plenty of notice of any funding requirement then they are more likely to give it to you.

EXERCISE

Go back through this chapter and write down what cash improvements you can implement in your business right now.

Real world thoughts

So often it's the profitable fast growing businesses that run out of cash. They are growing so fast that they can't get the cash in the door quick enough to pay for the extra team members, extra products or additional fixed costs that come with running a bigger business.

If they had raised funding or capped their growth for a period of time to get cash in their bank account to pay for the growth then they would be fine. But they didn't see themselves having a cash problem because they think 'cash isn't a problem for us because we are profitable and growing'.

Don't get me wrong, the loss making retracting businesses run out of cash too but that is expected. The owners of the profitable fast growing businesses don't expect to have a cash flow problem.

Cash management is about timing. Getting more cash in than is going out. It sounds simple and it is but so many businesses fall foul of this and have more cash going out than they have coming in. Mainly because they don't know their cash position and haven't put their growth plans through a cash flow forecast, which would spot any points in the future where cash would be tight.

Cash follows profit but to get profit you often need cash. That's why it is so important to understand your cash position and check your cash flow forecast before making big decisions.

To start with in my first business I had a cash flow problem because I didn't get on top of chasing the amounts customers owed me. I wouldn't get time to chase debts or I would put it off because it's a difficult conversation. Yet I had done the work and was rightly owed the money.

The interesting thing was I gave everyone thirty days to pay their invoice, some did and some didn't pay on time, but I had no reason to do this other than everyone else does it. I didn't credit check my customers to see if they were worthy of my credit or check to see if they are serial bad payers. I chose those payment terms because I thought that was the norm.

When I changed my payment terms to be paid monthly in advance most of the clients agreed to the terms and not surprisingly the bad payers decided to work with someone else.

This was a huge relief for me. Not only did I know that cash was coming in each month before the work was done but I didn't have to have difficult conversations with my customers. If the payment didn't come in I would have to speak with them but I was under no pressure because I hadn't completed any work so if they didn't pay they didn't get what they wanted.

In addition to slow paying customers the other reason cash is an issue for small businesses is that the owners take out more money than they are entitled to. This is either because of a mindset where they feel the money is theirs and not the money of the business. Or because they haven't checked the monthly figures or with their accountant to see how much money they can pay themselves.

The owner then gets used to a certain lifestyle so when they have to reduce their income from the business and possibly repay some cash, it's even harder to get the business cash position back to a positive.

CHAPTER SUMMARY

Key points

- The three main reasons for cash flow problems are not getting paid on time by your customers, paying yourself too much than the business can afford and not making enough profit.
- Review your payment terms and consider if bad payers should be put on cash upfront payment terms.
- Get better debt chasing and credit control procedures. Possibly outsource this.
- Consider getting paid in advance.
- Only pay your suppliers before the due date if there is a benefit to your business otherwise make use of the full payment terms. Don't pay late though.
- It's even more important to understand the cash position and forecast of your business when it is growing.
- Fund any cash short falls in the most cost effective way that also fit with your goals for the business.
- Make use of grants and subsidies to fund the growth of your business.

Exercise checklist

Get your twenty-four month budget and cash flow forecast at www.stevenbriginshaw.com/profitsbonus

Write down the cash improvements you can make in your business

TIME USAGE IMPROVEMENT

The more profit and cash you have in your business the more time you can save by paying someone to delegate or outsource to. But you can find time usage improvements by making small changes to how you and your team work.

From the packets of tea example you will remember that you can reduce your customer base saving you time as well as earning more profit for doing so. If you had less customers you would have more time. You will want to grow the business so you have more and more customers but you should make sure you are paid the right price for the work that you do.

Although you love what you do it is important to get harmony in your life, particularly with how you spend your time. The harmony doesn't need to be exactly equal in all areas of your life but there does need to be harmony, an agreement, with the time you spend in your business, your health, your family, your friends, your community and educating yourself. When you spend time in each of these areas of your life you will feel so much happier than if you were just spending all of your time in one area, which most likely will be your business.

It's while you are away from your business that you get the best ideas or find a solution to a problem because you have the time to think. You will also feel more energetic towards work after having a break or doing something that you enjoy.

Harmony is different to balance because you can spend a week travelling and working for business and not physically spend time with your family. But if your family understand why you are away for that week and that you have time booked in the diary to spend with them and away from the business then there is an agreement, a harmony between business and family. There clearly isn't balance because business is the main focus and there is no time with the family for that week. You can't have balance in all areas of your life all the time but you can have harmony.

Do only the things that you should do

As the business owner there will be certain things that only you should do such as goal planning, marketing, strategy planning, leading and motivating the team, reviewing your key numbers etc. So these are the things that you should spend your time on and nothing else. You want your team to do the technical work, the selling, the admin, the bookkeeping and all the other day to day tasks.

You may still need to complete some of the day to day tasks because your team isn't quite big enough or you haven't found the right suppliers to outsource but the ultimate goal of a business owner is to create a business that can run without you. Sure, you can still do some of the technical work or the selling if you enjoy it and have a CEO to do the business owner tasks, but you want the choice of being able to not do it and the business is still able to grow if you don't.

To give you an idea of what you can delegate or outsource you should go back to your hourly rate that you calculated earlier in the book.

Now list all of the tasks you complete each week. Go through your task list and ask yourself, 'can these be completed at a lower hourly rate than my hourly rate?' If the answer is 'yes' then delegate or outsource these tasks.

You should also use your task list to review if any tasks can be simplified or eliminated. You should simplify tasks so they take less of your time to complete or they can then be delegated or outsourced. Eliminate those tasks that don't really need to be done.

Spending your time in your business

The Urgent/Important matrix made famous by Stephen Covey helps you to work out what tasks you should be working on based on whether they are urgent or not and important or not.

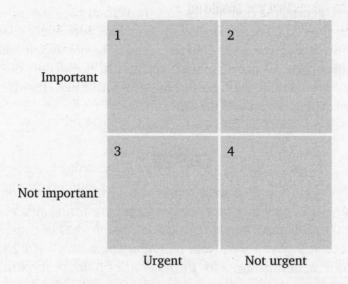

Urgent means that your attention is required immediately. Important means that it is essential to get you to where you want to go.

Quadrant one means it's important and urgent. An example is a problem, fire-fighting or a deadline. These tasks cannot be left otherwise your business will fall down. You should do these things now.

Quadrant two means it's important but not urgent. An example is goal planning or exercise. These tasks need to be done to accomplish your goals. You should plan time to do these.

Quadrant three means not important but urgent. An example is an interruption by certain emails, phone calls or attending certain meetings. These tasks tend to be urgent for other people and they want these tasks to be urgent for you as well. You should find a better way of doing these tasks or stop them before they happen by automating, delegating, simplifying, systemising or eliminating.

Quadrant four means not important and not urgent. An example is moving paper around, checking Facebook or chatting around the water cooler. These tasks tend to just kill time but in some circumstances can be used as a reward for working on quadrant two tasks. You should exclude these altogether from your working day.

THE PROFITS PRINCIPLES

The key to getting the right things done (quadrant two) is to schedule them and then do them first before anything else. Sometimes quadrant two items will become urgent but they tend to be not urgent and that is why this matrix is a powerful tool because you can identify the tasks you should be working on to get to your ideal future even though there is no real sign of urgency to do so.

EXERCISE

Analyse your time for a week seeing where you spend your time. Simply write each task that you do in the most fitting quadrant of the Urgent/Important matrix with the number of hours spent. For example if you were goal planning you would write that down in quadrant two with the amount of time spent on that task or if you were sending out sales invoices write that down in quadrant one with the time spent. If you are not sure which box a certain task should go into then just use your best guess. At the end of the week total up all of the hours spent in each quadrant.

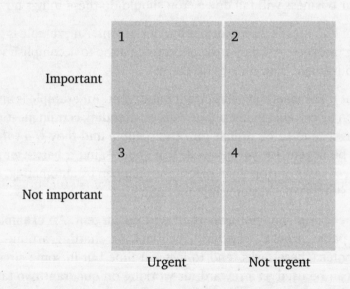

Once complete you will see what task you are doing, how much time you are spending on them and what quadrant of the Urgent/Important matrix you are spending most time in. You can then decide if that fits with what you should be doing and if not change how and what you work on.

You will probably find that you work most in quadrant one and quadrant three. Any time in your business that you spend in quadrant four can instantly be stopped saving you the total time for that box. Just don't do these tasks during the business day, save them for your down time or if you must do these tasks schedule these in to your day after quadrant two tasks are completed. Most importantly, try to schedule time so you can work on quadrant two tasks.

A week may sound like a long time, if it does just do this task for a day. However, you will get more insight and more results by sticking to the week. But once you have done it for one day you will be intrigued to see how the next day compares and will want to review the whole week. Also a week will typically include the core of the tasks you complete. To be certain you can review your analysis of your time spent in a week and list any missing tasks that you complete on a regular basis completing the same analysis.

To help you work on the right things you should plan in a diary your next day working in thirty or forty-five minute blocks by making appointments with yourself for the work that needs doing. So if you were going to work on your marketing first thing in the morning followed by a customer meeting then you would block out say ninety minutes in your diary at the start of your day for your marketing work, and block out the next say ninety minutes for the meeting. Once you have filled up all of your day you will know exactly what you will be working on.

Then at the end of each day you can review if you stuck to the appointments that you made, completed all the tasks that you were supposed to and check that you are working on the right things that will help you move closer to achieving your goals. You can then plan properly for the next day based on what you should do and what you didn't complete from the previous day. Instead of trying to find the time you will simply schedule it in your diary because when it is scheduled it will get done.

Get a template of the Urgent/Important matrix with a time tracker template from www.stevenbriginshaw.com/profitsbonus.

Work on the important tasks at the right time for you

You, like everyone else will have a time of day when you are in the zone. You have the most energy, you are most aware and most able to get things done. Ideas just pop out of your head, completed work seems to fly off of your desk and you enjoy doing the work as well as the satisfaction of getting it done.

This is your zone time and this time should be reserved for all of your important work.

The time of day this happens for you will be at the same time each day and will come in two or three waves. However, your zone time is specific to you and the same applies to everyone else, their zone time is specific to them. You will naturally be better at certain times of the day. Yes caffeine and other energy boosting supplements can help to artificially create your zone time but it isn't the same and it isn't sustainable to eat or drink things to achieve this.

Instead you should find when you are naturally at your best. For a week record your energy levels on a scale of one to ten every hour on the hour from when you wake to when you go to bed. It's best if you can avoid alcohol and caffeine during this time.

If your results are inconclusive then extend the zone time experiment for another week until you can start to see a pattern. Particularly if you are a moderate or heavy coffee or alcohol drinker you will need to do this experiment for longer as the caffeine and alcohol will most likely still be in your body and you will suffer withdrawal symptoms too that will mask your natural energy highs.

Also consider your quality and quantity of sleep because this will impact your energy levels. You will most likely have more energy and more mental clarity if you have had a restful eight hours sleep rather than a disturbed night or only, say, four hours' sleep.

What you will find is the time of day when you are in your zone and the time of day when you are in a slump.

Schedule your important task, and not replying to emails, for when you are naturally in your zone and schedule downtime or tasks that don't require much energy or thought when you are in a slump. Do pay attention to what you are eating and drinking as this can affect your quality and length of your zone time.

Get a template energy tracker from www.stevenbriginshaw.com/profitsbonus.

Real world thoughts

Improving how I use my time is one of the main areas I have focused on since I started my first business.

For me the biggest win was setting time aside each morning when I would work, uninterrupted and distraction free, on the tasks that would move me closer to my goals. This was instead of working on five things at once having my phone next to me, my email inbox open and not really having any focus at all.

Another big impact was only checking email at certain times during the day, and now on only certain days, instead of having the email notification on and checking emails throughout the day.

This time and focus discipline spilled over into my personal life too. I'm working towards doing only the things that I enjoy and want to do rather than need to do and giving those tasks to someone else in return for money or an appreciative hug. Things like washing the car, painting the garden fences, decorating the house, writing the food menu for the week and doing the ironing.

I'm really lucky because I don't have anything to do that I would consider a chore. I enjoy everything I do. Actually I still put the bins out, but I'm not sure I can outsource that one! This is a recent phenomenon for me though; it wasn't always this way and I have an amazing wife who helps me live life in my zone of enjoyment. Of course I do help around the house, but I enjoy doing those tasks – they are not chores to me.

Previously, I would work an eight hour day and then work a few more hours in the evenings. I would work both days at the weekend giving myself only a few hours of 'me' time to catch up with friends or watch a football match. Those days were really intense. Being busy doing lots of stuff but not really making any progress.

It took a few years to get from there to where I am now by following the principles in this book. I slowly got better, higher paying, customers and fewer of them. I changed how I worked and worked on the important non urgent tasks first. I delegated and outsourced the work I could. I used a planner to plan my day ahead. I took up meditation and practiced being more self-aware to better live in the present. I took time out of my day to rest, listen to music, go for a walk or nap even though it felt counterproductive and what I should be doing is slogging my guts out to get loads done.

In a nutshell, it was a mindset shift and persistent hard work, working on the right things, which got me to where I am now from the chaos that I used to live in.

There is absolutely no reason why you too can't get to a place where you enjoy doing everything that you do. If I can do it by using the principles in this book then you can too.

CHAPTER SUMMARY

Key points

- Aim for harmony in your life not work/life balance.
- Get time away from your business by having regular breaks during the day, weekends off and some time off on holiday.
- Do only the things you should do. Do only the things you enjoy. Delegate or outsource everything else that you are able to in your current situation.
- Schedule time to work on the important not urgent tasks first and stick to the schedule.
- Work on the important tasks at times when you naturally have the most energy.
- Work towards getting the mindset that you will only work on the things you enjoy and want to do.

Exercise checklist

Write down how you spent your time in the Urgent/Important matrix

Get an Urgent/Important matrix, time tracker template and energy tracker template at www.stevenbriginshaw.com/profitsbonus

SAVE TAX
Tax planning

There are plenty of things you can do to make sure you and your business are as tax efficient as possible. Things like having the best business structure, paying yourself from the business in the best way and getting the use of a car through the best way for you and your business.

The important thing is that it is the best way for you and your business. Every person and business are different so the best way for you may not be the best way for someone else. The two key words in tax are 'it depends'. It depends on your situation. It depends on what you want to achieve. It depends on the amounts involved. It depends on your cash flow and so on.

That is why it is crucial to sit down regularly with a really great accountant who understands you and your business and where you want to go so that the best tax planning for your situation can be put in place. By meeting regularly your accountant will then be able to recommend tax planning and other suggestions to improve your business without you having to ask for it because they will have a great understanding of what you want to achieve and what is currently going on in your business and in your life.

Timing is everything in tax so you need to speak to your accountant before you do anything. It is best to speak to them at the idea stage so they can best advise you on what to do. This is because the tax planning needs to be completed before you implement the idea. You cannot go back and change things once you have made the transaction.

For example if your business year-end is 31st March and you buy, on 31st March, new IT equipment for the office costing £10,000, your business will save £2,000 in corporation tax at 20% of the cost in that year-end. However, if you bought the same IT equipment on 1st April

215

you would have to wait a whole year to get the tax relief. It's true that if you are saving for your tax as you go each month then it won't have too much of an impact but if not then you've just lost £2,000 for a year.

Another example is if you decide to purchase a car in the company on hire purchase and only let your accountant know when you turn up at the office in your new car they will be pretty upset with you.

The reason is that you may have been better off from a tax and cash flow point of view to have a contract hire car and perhaps not in the company. Your accountant would be able to crunch the numbers to see the best way of getting your new car for your situation. But once the car has been purchased it's too late to change and you are stuck with the tax and cash consequences.

From time to time you will most likely hear from your friends and associates that they have done something to save tax and suggest you should do it too. Rather than take their advice and implement the same thing immediately, take that information to your accountant because you may already be saving tax in the same way or it may not be relevant to you and your business. Your accountant will be able to explain to you the full details.

There is a saying in the tax world. Don't let the tax tail wag the business dog. This means don't make decisions completely based on the tax savings. You need to look at the bigger picture and the business as a whole. You need to consider how the tax decision will affect how your business operates and makes money. How it will affect your cash flow now and in the future. All the things you would consider for a normal business decision need to be considered when looking at tax planning, in addition to how much tax the planning will save and if it is cost effective. And you will want to include the tax impact when making all business decisions.

To get access to the right tax planning you will need to work with a good accountant who has a network of tax experts specialising in different areas of tax or has all of these experts in their business. You can then be sure that your accountant will bring the right tax planning to you before you have to ask for it.

Tax planning also involves your family. Your parents and grandparents, your spouse or partner, your children and grandchildren. This could be tax planning for them individually and how it affects you or it can be how your tax planning will affect them.

Tax planning also involves your team as there could be an impact on them and if you are as tax efficient as possible then your team should be as well.

There are certain tax planning opportunities that are only available to you if you have a certain amount of income or your business has a certain amount of profit. This is because of the costs involved in the advice and implementation of the tax planning. Tax planning must always be cost effective, so you save more tax than it costs you for the advice. You wouldn't save tax of £5,000 if it cost you £7,000 for the advice. Generally in life, the more money you have the more opportunity you have to make more money. This also applies to saving tax.

It is the job of a great accountant to make you aware of what tax planning is available for your situation regardless of your accountant's view on the tax planning. Your accountant shouldn't prejudge or preselect the relevant tax planning they bring to you. Instead they should bring all of the relevant and legal tax planning options to you and let you decide what you want to do based on how it fits with your financial, risk and moral profiles.

You will have your own view on tax which will most likely be linked to your view of the world. You will either want to pay as much as possible to ensure the country benefits from the services provided by tax payers, you will want to pay as little tax as legally possible or you will fit somewhere in between. Your tax morality is very important when deciding what tax planning you will do. But only you will know this as you may change your attitude or your current circumstances may cause a change in your view. Your accountant will need to ask you at the right time and so the best way to do this is to present you with all of the relevant legal tax planning available and give you the facts so you can make an informed decision.

There are risks with everything in life and as a business owner you are taking risks everyday so you are in a good position to understand that there too are risks involved with tax planning. Most tax planning has a low or very low element of risk but some tax planning will have a higher degree of risk. Again this all depends on your risk profile as you may be a risk taker or completely against risk. So your accountant also needs to give you the facts about the risks involved with the relevant legal tax planning. This risk will be: financial – can you and the business afford it; business – how it will affect your ability to trade as you currently are, and; tax – will the authorities want to know more about the tax planning.

Illegal and abusive tax planning should be avoided at all times regardless of your profile towards risk and tax morality. If the tax planning is illegal you will be prosecuted. If the tax planning is abusive you will breach legislation and face prosecution. You will most likely also be fined, asked to pay the tax that you saved through illegal or abusive planning and suffer the cost and time wasted on the investigations and court appearances.

You should trust your accountant not to bring this type of tax planning to you because their professional body (assuming they are registered with a professional accountancy body – check this with them) will not allow them to do so. But you can apply these two rules to tax planning regardless of your risk, moral and financial profiles:

If it is complicated to understand the process or where the money goes, then don't do it. If it sounds dodgy or you are not comfortable with it, then don't do it.

You can download a help sheet to finding a great accountant at www.stevenbriginshaw.com/profitsbonus.

The best time to plan for tax

There are a few key times each year when you should be sitting down with your accountant to review the progress of the year to date, the tax impact of that and then how to plan for tax for the months ahead.

As well as the timing of the transaction, the timing of tax planning is the key to saving thousands of pounds in tax or paying thousands of pounds extra in tax. The main message is you need to plan for tax before the situation arises. The next most important message is that you need to speak with your accountant at that time to get the expert help you need to get the details right to make sure you are not paying any more tax than you have to pay.

Generally two months before the transaction or cut-off date is a good time to start tax planning as this gives plenty of time to understand the situation, make a decision and put into action any steps that you need to in order to pay tax more efficiently.

At least two months before the year-end of your business so you can make sure you get the right things in the current financial year and in the next financial year. It's surprising but one day will have a dramatic effect on the tax your business pays and on your business cash flow.

For example, it is near your business year-end date and you are about to purchase £20,000 of equipment to help your business serve your customers better and to enable you to work more efficiently. So do you want to make the purchase on or before the year-end or after the year-end date? At a tax rate of 20% you would save £4,000 of tax on this purchase. You would definitely want to make this purchase before the end of your business year-end otherwise you would have to wait twelve months before you could get the tax relief of £4,000 for the purchase. One day has a twelve month cash flow effect. A simple decision isn't it. But if you are not thinking about it you could quite easily let the purchase run over a day or two particularly if the supplier is late with their paperwork or with the delivery, etc.

This is just one example but it shows how simple decisions should be made but you need to take the time out of your business to think about it and plan with your accountant.

In the example above it is really just a cash flow timing but for other areas of tax planning it could mean the difference between saving tax and not saving tax, particularly if legislation is changing.

These principles apply to your individual tax position as well as for the business. Planning for tax personally at least two months before the personal tax year-end is a great time to ensure that you have time to get the right things done.

For any ideas you have that will change circumstances in your business, in your personal life or that have a financial impact you should always discuss these ideas with your accountant at this stage, before any action is taken. Speaking to your accountant after you have made the change or transaction will simply be an information exercise because if you didn't take the right steps there is nothing your accountant can do. Changes can't be made retrospectively.

You may purchase a car in your company through a hire purchase agreement, but if you didn't speak with your accountant before you made the purchase how do you know it was the right thing to do? Should you have purchased the car personally instead? Or should you have got a loan, a lease or contract hire? It seems simple enough to purchase a new car but the tax implications for you and your business are much more complicated.

You may have moved your business from being a sole trader to a limited company. How did you know this was the right time to make the change? What is the tax effect of the change? Did you put all the necessary steps in place to get the best outcome for you and your business?

These are just two examples that seem simple enough decisions but each have a tax aspect that needs to be thoroughly considered to make sure you save as much tax as possible and don't pay any more tax than you have to pay.

Save for your tax

It is always the right thing to do to save for all taxes in your business. But to do this you need up-to-date figures on the performance of the business so you can instantly see how much available money you have in your business current account to spend on running the business, paying yourself extra or for growing the business.

Depending on your business structure, whether it is a sole trader, partnership or limited company, will determine the tax rate used to calculate how much tax you need to save each month. The general rule of thumb to calculate the tax amount to save each month is to multiply the tax rate with your monthly profits. This gives a quick, easy and fairly accurate estimate of your tax bill.

There are certain expenses that are not tax deductible such as customer entertaining, some legal fees and depreciation of IT equipment, furniture, vehicles and machinery. If doing the tax calculation properly non-tax deductible costs would need to be added back to the profit figure. In addition, any amounts spent on IT equipment, furniture and machinery will most likely receive tax relief on the full amount spent but these costs aren't included in the profit figure because they are considered assets, which are included on the balance sheet report. Tax relief on vehicles is more complex and possibly can be fully tax deductible or possibly just a small percentage of the cost will be tax deductible. You can see why it is simpler just to use the rule of thumb.

Whichever way you calculate the tax to save each month you will need to be working with a great bookkeeper who will help you get your monthly figures prepared accurately and within a month to know the amount of profit made for the month. The bookkeeper will also most likely calculate and tell you what to save each month for tax.

This will also give you peace of mind that your business can pay the tax when it is due without having to borrow money or impact on the trading of your business. You don't need to worry about finding the money. Just knowing you have the tax saved separately away from everything else gives an enormous relief. You have the cash to pay all taxes as and when they fall due. That's a pretty cool position to be in and it frees up your mind to focus on working on your business instead of worrying about money.

The money that you save should be earning your business as much of a return as possible. Some of the tax that you save will be required to be paid soon after it is saved but some tax may not be required for a year so speak with your bank manager to make sure the money is working as hard as it can to get the best return for your business.

You should also take the same approach for your personal tax to make sure you have the tax available when it is due without having an impact on your lifestyle and cost of living. With the comfort of knowing you are getting a good return for the savings.

Real world thoughts

As a trained chartered accountant saving tax is a natural thing for me to consider. If you aren't a chartered accountant then find a good one to help give you great tax advice before you realise you need it. They are out there you just need to know where to look.

At the minimum, use the information in this chapter to help you consider tax planning.

If you do hear a great tax tip from someone down the pub or at your local sports club then get clarity on the tax advice from the accountant that gave the tip to that person. Don't believe 100% what the person has told you before speaking to a tax adviser. Lots of people get caught up taking advice from their friends or colleagues when it turns out the advice wasn't quite right for their situation or what they told you was only half of the story.

The timing of tax planning is critical that's why it's really important to speak with your accountant before making any big decisions like buying high priced equipment, getting a new car, gifting money to family members and buying a holiday home. Once the transaction has taken place you can't go back and change things to save tax.

I know of a business owner that purchased a car with a personal contract hire agreement but, with his particular circumstances, had he spoken with his accountant he would have found a more tax and cash flow efficient way of getting the car through the business on contract hire.

I also heard of a situation where a business owner transferred shares in her company to her boyfriend to save tax but that triggered a Capital Gains tax payment on the sale of the shares even though there were no funds paid to her for the shares. What they didn't realise was they need to be married for there not to be a Capital Gains tax charge at the time of transferring the shares. This was on the advice of a family friend who either didn't know the full details of the tax planning or didn't know her marital status.

The one tax that I always see overlooked is Inheritance Tax and normally the business owners who haven't considered Inheritance Tax haven't got a will either, which is simply madness especially if they have young children. In 80% of cases no tax planning is needed but it gives peace of mind to get it done. The other 20% should take tax advice and decide what is best for them and their family but they don't know they are one of the 20% because they don't think about planning for Inheritance Tax.

It could be because Inheritance Tax is paid when the business owner passes away so maybe they don't like thinking about their own death or maybe they don't care because they won't be around when the tax needs to be paid. For whatever reason writing a will and planning for Inheritance Tax are not done by business owners.

Another area that I see overlooked is saving for tax to be able to pay it when it falls due. This is such a basic thing yet so many business owners don't save for their tax bills. This is corporation tax, personal tax, VAT and PAYE. It's liberating and allows you to focus your energy on more important matters when you know you have all of the tax money set aside in a deposit account ready to pay when it is due.

CHAPTER SUMMARY

Key points

- Find a great accountant to give you tax advice.
- Every person and business are different so get tax advice specific to your circumstances.
- Timing is everything in tax so speak with your accountant as early as possible before making big decisions.
- Consider the commercial, cash flow and other implications before following tax advice. Don't just do something for the tax saving if it will have a knock on effect somewhere else.
- Understand your tax morality and don't enter into tax planning that goes against it.
- Before the end of the business accounting year and before the end of the personal tax year are great times to complete tax planning.
- Save monthly for all of your taxes in separate deposit accounts for peace of mind and to have the funds available when the taxes are due.

Exercise checklist

Get a help sheet to find a great accountant at www.stevenbriginshaw.com/profitsbonus

SYSTEMISE YOUR BUSINESS
The ultimate goal

The ultimate goal of a business owner is to create a profitable business that can run without you and grow as well. This is what every business owner should be aiming for otherwise you simply just own a job. A job means that when you stop working so too does the income stop coming.

With a systemised business and a team to follow the systems you can choose what you want to work on in or outside of the business. You may love sales or some of the technical work that you do so you will want to keep on doing that with a CEO in place to run the business or you may want to start another business or sail around the world or simply spend time with your family. The point is it is your choice. You are in control and have the power to choose what you want to be, do or have.

Essentially your business is just a collection of systems and people. Systems to get every function in your business to produce the same consistent result every single time. And people to follow, create, maintain and remove systems to get those results. That's all it comes down to and you will need to see your business in this way, a collection of moving parts like a machine with people to operate it to get the desired end result.

Like most business owners you will want your perfect work/life harmony. You may choose to have a two week holiday with your family without being interrupted by work. Or you may want two days a week to spend on your hobbies. And you may want to maintain or improve the money you get paid from your business for your lifestyle without you having to work all hours for it. The best way to get these is to systemise your business, accomplish the ultimate goal.

The only way to achieve the ultimate goal is through systemisation. Creating systems in your business that your team can follow to get the same great result each and every time. Whether that is answering the telephone, delivering technical work or having a sales meeting. You will need a system for everything that you do in your business.

A system is simply, 'the way you do things'. A step by step guide of how to complete a task in a certain way that gives the desired result each and every time.

Your business will not be totally dependent on any one person whether that is you or a key team member. If you or they are not at work for any reason the business can still function and produce the right results. The systems will be out of your head and written down so anyone with the right training for the task can follow it.

Systems will allow growth to happen naturally, because process is hardwired into your business and in everything that your team does.

This doesn't happen overnight and it takes a lot of hard work either working through yourself, with your team or bringing in a systems expert. You and your team will need to regularly test and measure each system to make sure it is doing what it should be and that it is up to date. Then test and measure the improvements that you make. Things will change in and outside of your business so your systems will need to change with these too.

There will be stages in your business for you wanting to systemise your business. First when you work on your own to make sure that you aren't forgetting to do certain tasks and get the consistent results for your customers.

After this, when you take on your first team members so they know what and how to produce the right results every single time for the tasks they will complete.

Next, when you need more time to spend on strategy and growing the business so you bring in or outsource some of the technical work that you do. You will take yourself away from the day to day running of the business to focus on long term goals and leading and motivating your team.

Then when you want you spend more time doing things outside of the business. When you bring in a CEO to handle the high level tasks you were doing. You then have the time to do the things that you love inside and outside of the business with the knowledge that the business will continue to get the same great results over and over again as well as adapt to change and innovate.

Systems allow you to grow or scale the business up or down very quickly so you can adapt and react quickly to changes, create new services or have new locations.

You and your team will use a system each time a task is required, which will ensure consistent results for your business and highlight any areas to improve or change.

Having a systemised business will make it easier to sell, get you a higher price and more favourable terms, simply because the purchaser can just follow the systems to get the same results as you. Or will make it easier for those who will run your business for you to continue to get the same great results without your input.

Work/life harmony not balance

In the previous section you may have expected to read work/life balance instead of work/life harmony but balance at all times isn't possible. You may be on a four day conference with work so your work focus is heavier than your focus on family and friends, on your community, possibly even on your health and hobbies. Or you may be on a two week family holiday so your focus on family is much heavier than your focus on work. Balance means an even distribution or a steady position and in these examples there isn't one as one area of your life has taken more of the distribution of your energy. The scales of the areas of your life are not evenly balanced.

Harmony is easier to achieve and maintain. Harmony means being in a state of agreement which provides a consistent whole, in other words, having all the areas of your life in agreement to provide a happy and fulfilled you. The agreement is that balance cannot always be maintained and that all areas of your life will get enough of your energy over a period of time to make you happy and fulfilled in each area of your life. Even if you have unbalanced focus in your life, like being on a four day work conference or being on a two week family holiday, you can still have harmony. But only as long as you are aware that your energy is focused on one particular area of your life, that you are happy and fulfilled and that you have a plan shared with those involved in your life that you will focus your energy on the other areas within an agreed period of time.

System Champion

To make sure all of the systems in your business are like the parts of a well-oiled machine you will need someone to watch over the parts, make repairs, changes and oil it where and when needed. Someone who is responsible for keeping the machine running at its optimal rate and output. This someone is a Systems Champion.

Appoint someone who is good at following systems, is logical and has an open mind to be your Systems Champion. This may even be you to start with and if it is make sure that you appoint someone in your growing team to take over this role from you.

They will train the rest of your team on how to use systems and what to do if there are breaks in the systems or updates required. Also they will be able to get feedback from the team to amend existing systems and create new systems.

You want your whole team to write, improve or challenge systems in your business but your Systems Champion will review and approve the systems in your business before setting them live for everyone to use.

If something goes wrong in your business it is the responsibility of the system and not of the person following it. Remember you must take ultimate responsibility for the team you work with so make sure they can follow systems and make sure your Systems Champion can write easy to follow systems and can fix broken systems.

You and your team will all need access to your business systems so it is best to store them centrally in one place where everyone can get access to them at the same time but they are secure enough to stop anyone outside of the business gaining access.

You may want to store them on a computer or a server which is regularly backed up to ensure if the server fails then you haven't lost your business. Or you can access your systems online via a cloud solution that does all the backing up for you so all you need is an internet connection, email address and password.

How to systemise

Below, to get you started on systemising your business, is a basic step by step guide. Ideally you will need to complete steps one and two, either on your own or with your team and, preferably, your team will complete step three. The steps need to be completed in order; so you cannot jump to step three without first completing steps one and two. The reason for this is to make sure step three is consistent with the previous steps. I really believe in the process in Sam Carpenter's *Work the System* and the steps below are my take on how to systemise.

Earlier in the book we considered the ideal endgame options for your business being to sell it, keep it and earn income while doing what you love or pass it on to family. You will remember that each endgame requires the same ingredient; systemisation. You will also remember that through the book systemisation is mentioned to get the same great result every time. Here's how to do it.

Step One – Identify and write down your Purpose
Your purpose is your ideal identity for your business, the direction you wish to move towards and how you operate. Your purpose will help guide you and your team to fulfil your goals. It will help create the correct mindset for everyone involved with your business and will be used as a double check measure in decision making by asking the question, 'does my decision agree with the purpose of the business?'

This will start simply as you want to be the best at something that is measurable in your sector or industry in your location. For example, if you worked in digital recruitment in Hampshire your purpose may start with, 'We are the best digital recruitment firm in the UK at placing the most candidates with the highest gross profit per employee'.

You may not be able to get the results of your competitors to compare against but you will most likely be able to get hold of results for the top 100 businesses in your industry. So for the example above the results of the digital recruitment companies in the UK may not be available but the results of the top 100 recruitment firms in the UK will be. In any case you don't necessarily need to compare to your competitors, your purpose is to keep improving your results to make your business the best it can be. You are competing with yourself, constantly making small improvements.

Your purpose needs to be written in present tense. This is really important as it makes you and your team believe you are already there, even if you are not. So you start thinking and acting like the best.

Your purpose will also need to include details about what your business does, what makes your business unique, the specific markets/industries you serve and how you and your team will become and remain the best. The reason for having so much detail is so that anyone reading your purpose will instantly understand what you and your business stand for, who you work with, what you do and where you are going.

Your purpose isn't a fluffy mission statement that everyone forgets about. Your purpose is the key to making decisions in your business for you and your team.

To help write the purpose for your business you will need to pick up from earlier in the book when you were thinking about your why and your purpose in life. You may simply want to be the best at what you do in your location and that is great. Whatever it is, you and your team must have this at the forefront of your mind for every task you complete, every conversation over the phone or email you have, and how you behave in and outside of your workplace.

If you are stuck for ideas on what the purpose of your business should be then these questions may help.
- What do you want your business to be known for?
- What one thing does your business need to be good at to succeed?
- Why did you start the business in the first place?

The nutshell purpose of my UK-wide bookkeeping business is we are the best bookkeeping and management reporting business in the UK at producing easy to understand monthly reports with guaranteed turnaround times and the highest customer satisfaction score.

We exist to give every business owner in the UK the key information they need, in plain English, so they can make quick and fact based simple decisions to move towards their goals.

Step Two – Identify and write down your Values

Your business values are closely linked to your personal values as essentially your business is an extension of your personality. Your values are the standards you expect of yourself and expect of others and the beliefs you hold dear to your heart. Your business takes on your personality, beliefs and values but it is completely separate from you. If you want to create a business that can run and potentially be sold without you, then you cannot be the business and the business cannot be you.

Your values help you to fulfil your purpose. They give the expectation of how to think and act in your business for you and your team.

The values are like the rules of the game. The game is your business and the rules define how the game is played or in other words how your business is run.

To write the values of your business you will start with your beliefs. What do you fundamentally believe as a person? Do you believe that everyone needs to be their authentic self, that the 80/20 principle is everywhere or what goes around comes around?

What are your beliefs in your business? Do you believe that the customer comes first, that everyone should be open and honest, that mistakes are a good thing as long as a lesson is learned and that work should be fun?

Next write down all of your expectations. Your expectations of yourself, your team, your customers, your suppliers and of your business in general. This will include things like how you expect people to communicate with each other, how you expect people to work, how you expect people to react to certain situations and how you expect people to behave when working with your business.

Finally, write down the mindset that your team will need to have to do what you want them to do and how they should interact with your customers.

Your values will be linked closely to your ideal customer and your ideal team member because you will want to work with people who share the same values as you. In turn, they will be attracted to you because they share the same values.

Your business purpose and values are essential to get completed before you dive into writing your processes so definitely spend the time thinking about and writing them first. They are like the foundations for building a house. You cannot build a sturdy, successful and functional building without foundations. It would subside, fall apart and even collapse on the owner. It's the same for a business, these documents are the foundations for your business. No matter how tempted you are to get started on your procedures make sure the purpose and culture are written and explained to your team first.

The purpose and culture are not just pieces of paper so once you have written them make sure you share them with your team. Get their feedback and input. You need to make sure that your team buy into them and that they understand the system mentality of your business.

Step Three – Document and follow your Procedures

Your procedures are what needs to be done, who it needs to be done by and how it needs to be done. You may also call these your processes or systems in your business.

To get you started on identifying your procedures, write down on a blank piece of paper all of the work you currently complete.

Then write next to those tasks a 'Yes' if you can delegate/outsource it, which may require some training, or a 'No' if it is not possible for anyone else to complete those tasks other than you.

Earlier in the book you reviewed your time spent over a week and allocated an IN or an ON depending on whether the task completed was working IN your business or ON your business. Add all of these tasks to your list and if you found IN tasks that you want to delegate or outsource then put a 'Yes' next to them.

For all of the 'Yes' answers rank the top three that take up the majority of your time and energy.

Now you can start writing the procedures of these tasks, starting with the one that takes up most of your time and energy, so you can delegate or find a supplier to outsource those tasks. With the extra time and energy you now have you can continue to systemise the rest of your business, one task at a time.

To write the procedure you can simply document what you are doing as you complete the task. Or better still work with the person you are delegating or outsourcing to and ask them to write the process as you teach them what to do.

You can document this by taking notes, speaking into a voice recorder on your phone or using screen capture software to create a video with you speaking into a headset explaining what you are doing at each step. You can also get the voice recording or video transcribed so there is a written document to compliment the voice recording or video. Also by having video, audio and text of the process you can cater for every learning style of your team. Some of your team will learn best by seeing so reading the text or watching the video will be best for them. Some of your team will learn best by listening so hearing the video or voice recording will be best of them. And some of your team will learn best getting hands on and will refer to either the text, audio or video when they need help. Store the text, audio and video files somewhere safe, that is backed up regularly, and where the right people can access it.

Once the procedure is documented start following it immediately and for each and every time the task needs completing. Remember you don't want people to store things in their heads, you want them to follow the system. To help encourage your team to do so you can explain that as long as the system is followed no team member will take the blame for something going wrong, it will be the process that is blamed. This should be one of your values.

Don't worry about getting the procedure 100% on the first time. There are likely to be things that you missed and things will change in the future. Each time that you or a team member follow a process and there appears to be a step or some information missing then simply update the process. The process is a living breathing thing that will evolve as your business evolves. You can give your team the authority to update the process as long as they follow the purpose and values of your business and then report the changes to the appropriate people maybe in a team meeting.

Another procedure that should be near the top of your priority list for writing procedures is the procedure to create procedures. This is so your team can follow the procedure to write the procedures for their role and any other tasks you ask them to write procedures for. The more hands on deck the easier and quicker it will be. You will also eventually need the procedure to write procedures anyway so it makes sense to do it at the beginning.

When working on your procedures take the long term view and spend an hour a day or a few hours a week to move towards having a fulfilling systemised business that can run without you. You are working hard anyway so work hard on the right things that will bring you rewards every year rather than working on fire fighting and only getting breathing space until the next issue. Work hard on the right things and get well rewarded with your time and money or work really hard on everything else and in a year's time be in the same position or worse.

Your team will need to actively follow the purpose, culture and procedures in your business and this is something the System Champion will need to work on to make sure each team member is doing so. If your team don't buy into these documents then they will not use them. Anybody that doesn't understand why you use systems and isn't prepared to follow your procedures shouldn't be part of your team. They will be a bad influence on your other team members and will slow down your progress.

The payback for your time and effort you spend on writing your business purpose, values and procedures will be huge. It will enable you to free up your time by passing the day to day work on to the team who will be able to produce the same consistent results as you by following all three documents. With this time you can then work ON your business more which will result in more sales, more profit, more efficiency, more share of your market and more help to those you want to help. You will enjoy your work and make more money simply by doing the right things in your business and for all those connected with your business. You will step into the virtuous circle of ever recurring rewards.

Download your template purpose, values and procedure documents from www.stevenbriginshaw.com/profitsbonus.

This last chapter on systemisation brings all of the other parts of the **PROFITS** principles, from the previous chapters, together neatly in a gift wrapped box. It's a beautiful gift for you because you are now able to spend your time doing the things you love within and outside of your business.

Also, it's a beautiful gift to a potential buyer because all they need to do is to follow the systems, they don't really need you, which is great as you are unlikely to have in the sale agreement a long period of working for the purchaser and you are unlikely to have a big part of the sale price paid out upon targets you have to reach while working for them.

In other words, if you do sell your business after implementing all of the chapters in this book you will sell your business at a higher price, you will receive the majority of that price upfront and you won't need to work with the purchaser for long at all. Giving you the money and time to pursue your next venture or project.

After implementing all of these steps in your business you will find that more money and more time are a by-product, it just happens through working on the right things in your business. Once you've achieved success in each of the **PROFITS** Principles revisit it again because life and business are constantly changing and you will find something new that you didn't spot before.

Invest your time, energy and money wisely and follow the **PROFITS** Principles in this book to create the business of your dreams. The more you can invest in these principles the quicker you will get to your ideal future and the quicker you will take those small steps forward to your end destination.

Have fun, stay focused and keep moving.

Real world thoughts

The thought of systemising my business really sunk in when I read Michael Gerber's *The E-Myth Revisited*. I was able to take what I had in my head already and form a complete puzzle picture with his direction.

I saw how each process made up each department and each department made up the business. The processes being the nuts, bolts and cogs in the machine and the people to run, maintain and improve the machine are the team members in the business.

The biggest learning, though, was that I shouldn't be doing everything in my business, I should have systems, processes and a team to help me achieve my vision.

It all made sense. Write systems to get the same results every single time. Bring in capable people who can follow, maintain and improve the systems. Lead and manage the people. Build great relationships with your customers.

That book completely changed my life!

From that moment on I worked towards building a business that could run without me instead of a business that was completely dependent on me.

In my accountancy practice the first tasks I systemised were the tasks I could delegate or outsource. I wrote systems for handling my emails, for handling the post, for booking meetings and for the less involved technical work, the stuff that didn't need me to do it, it could be done by anyone with the right system.

This freed up so much of my time it was liberating! It then became addictive because you want to systemise everything.

I also wrote systems for the work that only I could do like signing off accounts, giving tax advice and running a strategy meeting. This enabled me to not have to think about what I was doing or what I had to do next, it was all on a process sheet or checklist, which made me so much more efficient and the work more enjoyable. I then had more time and space in my head to think about how to better delight my customers and to do the things I enjoyed.

As things progressed I asked the team to write the processes and check with me once complete. With any process, regardless of who had written it, we always tested it in real life by using the process and made amendments where needed.

When my daughter was born I took all day Friday off work to spend with her and did this for the first eleven months of her life. I was only able to take off Fridays because I had a systemised business and a team who knew how to work the systems.

My wife and I made the decision for me to go back to work on Fridays to move the business to the next level, which would help the whole family and was worth the sacrifice of not spending an extra day a week with my daughter.

There were times on Fridays when I thought I would rather be with my daughter than working but the decision we made paid off in the end.

Something else that helped me was my systemised diary. I allocated particular work for each day of the week. For example on a Monday I answered emails, made calls and completed some technical work. On a Tuesday I had meetings with clients and prospective clients. Wednesday was emails and technical work. Thursdays was client strategy meetings all day. On Friday I spent time with my daughter.

But each day, before doing anything I always worked on the tasks that would get me towards my goals. Tasks like systemisation, writing content for marketing, planning, working on new services and products, learning and checking the business performance against my goals and working out what to do next.

Although I always strived for work life balance, I was never able to achieve complete balance all of the time. It was very frustrating and I felt like a failure. I would also do things in a cycle. When I felt sluggish and unhealthy I would balance the scales representing health by focusing on eating well and exercising three to five times per week. The weights would then fall off my family and friends scale so I spent more time socialising and being present for my family. Then work would need more of my attention so I would focus my energy there. Then I would feel sluggish and overweight and unhappy so I would focus on my health again. Can you see the cycle?

It was soul-destroying and unbearable. So I decided to get off the scales for good and live in harmony instead. With harmony each area of my life is in a state of agreement with the others. I make small amounts of time available each day or week to cover most areas of my life. It feels energising and refreshing and is a much better place than trying to balance all of the scales at the same time.

I found it really hard not to jump straight into Step Three of systemising my business and in fact did write some procedures before writing the purpose and values of my business. But I then had to rewrite those procedures because they didn't line up with what I really wanted to achieve.

The purpose of my business was the hardest thing to come up with because it involved a lot of thought and interaction to understand what our customers want. Once written, it felt a little weird when reading it back but it gives a clear picture to everyone that reads it whether that is me, the team, our customers or suppliers. It also creates a certain mindset of asking, 'what would the best look like?' The rest is left up to yours and your customers' imagination.

The values flow much more easily from the purpose because it's how you believe you should act to fulfil your purpose. It takes time to write these and you will find that you add more values at later dates.

Once you have these down on paper it then gives you a clear picture on what procedures to write, how they should be written and what extra steps, with consideration of your purpose and values, to include.

It all takes time but it is so worth the effort.

CHAPTER SUMMARY

Key points

- The only way to build a profitable business that can run without you is to systemise your business. A business not dependent on any one person.
- A systemised business allows for the same consistent results to be delivered every time with anyone in the team capable of following the system.
- Systemised businesses sell for a higher price compared to a non-systemised business.
- Work towards work/life harmony not work/life balance.
- A Systems Champion will look after the systems in your business.
- How to systemise: Step one – Identify and write down your purpose
- How to systemise: Step two – Identify and write down your values
- How to systemise: Step three – Document and follow your procedures

Exercise checklist

Get template purpose, values and procedure documents at www.stevenbriginshaw.com/profitsbonus

NEXT STEPS

Thank you for reading the book and getting this far. Please make sure you visit www.stevenbriginshaw.com/profitsbonus to download templates, tips and help from the chapters of the book. These will help you get started on your success journey.

If you are stuck or have hit a plateau on your business journey and need some help then check out www.stevenbriginshaw.com/products. There are a range of ways to help to suit you, plus I can introduce you to an accountant who will help you understand your numbers and make better decisions.

If you are an accountant then visit www.clarity-hq.com to see how we at Clarity can help your firm and your clients with what's in this book, plus much, much more. Connect with me at www.stevenbriginshaw.com to read and comment on my blog posts and get links for my social media accounts to say hi and let me know about your business journey.

CASE STUDIES

During my career so far I have been fortunate enough to work with many amazing entrepreneurs. But the next three clients I will tell you about are very special and they have great businesses.

Sharon Dunne

When I first met Sharon I was impressed by her story so far. Her journey started as an employed dental Practice Manager who had to work really hard to keep the dental practice fully staffed, because team members were frequently not in work due to leave, holiday or sickness. So she came up with a solution to supply dental practices with temporary team members and through her own ambition and determination built the business from just her, initially, to 186 team members and fourteen managers.

Impressively after just a few years in business Sharon and her team won the prestigious Investor in People Award (Bronze) demonstrating their commitment to finding great team members and looking after them, who in turn deliver a great service to their clients.

But the two main reasons we were meeting was to help plug a cash flow hole because the rapid growth of the business had taken its toll on the bank balance. And to free up some time for Sharon who was working harder and longer hours than ever.

I started telling Sharon about the **PROFITS** Principles and she instantly got it. She could see right away that cash follows profit and that we needed to focus on her key metrics, the key areas that drive success in her business, and link them to her goals to improve the cash flow of the business. She could also see that profit was key to helping her to delegate some of her tasks to new team members.

We worked on why clients use her business, increased prices to reflect their superior service, created ways to motivate and incentivise the

243

team through monthly measurement of key metrics and created a long term business strategy to work towards and check against.

We've been working together since July 2013 and the results speak for themselves. At the time of writing these are the results of Sharon's and her teams' hard work:

Sales have increased by 123% to £2.2m. Gross profit has increased by 292% and net profit increased by 3043%. Almost unbelievable right! These guys work extremely hard and extremely well. To get these results the team has increased by 138% and the management team has increased by 40%.

As a result of the growth and tighter cash control the net cash position of the business has increased by 1085%.

Sharon's personal income has increased by 70% and we've saved her over £26,500 in tax by being more tax efficient. Sharon now has more time to spend with her husband and travel to more destinations than before, through delegation and making sure she leaves the office at 5pm. This is instead of her husband not really knowing who she is because of the late nights and weekends that she was working.

Sharon's business is now the stand-out leader in her industry and still continues to grow throughout the UK.

A remarkable lady, team and business.

Adam Cox

Adam and I first met at the Key Person of Influence programme that started in 2012 but it wasn't until the latter stages of the programme that we started to get to know each other. There were fifty people in our group, but we eventually got round to speaking to each other.

When Adam and I did speak we instantly clicked. It was like we had been friends for ages instead of only a few weeks. The more we got to know each other the more we realised we had in common.

We both are Liverpool FC fans, love performance cars, especially the Aston Martin DB9, love music, play the guitar and enjoy a trip to the cinema. We're both similar types of people; the biggest difference is that Adam comes from a health point of view and I come from a business point of view. Most interestingly, deep down, we both were facing similar internal challenges and obstacles.

I was also amazed and inspired by Adam's story so far. He left his life in Hull to move to London with nothing but a change of clothes. He built a successful and extremely profitable personal trainer business but realised that wasn't his calling and enrolled on the C.H.E.K. Institute training programme. Adam is now one of the top C.H.E.K. practitioners in the UK and he mentors other trainees.

It felt like we were destined to meet so it was only natural that we would help each other.

Adam, being a holistic wellbeing coach, helped me and still does, to become as healthy as I can from a spiritual, emotional, mental and physical perspective. We both believe that if we are as close to optimal health as we can be then we will function better in all areas of life and enjoy life as we are supposed to enjoy it. I also wanted to squeeze back into my old thirty-one-inch jeans.

I helped Adam move his business towards where he envisioned it to be from owning a job working on a time for money basis to owning a business and doing only the things in it that he loves to do while he and his team are paid well for the life changing work they do.

When we first started working together, Adam was working lots of hours and felt trapped on a treadmill, unable to get off or move forwards without working even more hours. His health was suffering as a result. He was making money but not what his skill set, and what he believed, was worth.

Adam owned a job and was working on a time for money basis without being able to see how to improve his situation, but he did notice his situation needed to change. He was working five and a half days, totalling at least fifty hours, per week, with just enough income to pay the bills and keep a small amount of profit aside for when and if the business needed it.

After our first session together Adam got huge clarity on his endgame vision not just for his business but for his ideal life. This provided the backbone to our sessions as we worked closer to his ideal future.

We worked on his service packages, his pricing, how he uses his time, who his ideal client is and what roles he really loves in his business. Taking the required parts from the **PROFITS** Principles and applying them to his situation.

The changes Adam has implemented in the first twelve months of working together are amazing. He has been able to cut down the hours he works to five days, totalling thirty-five hours, per week, two days of which are dedicated to working ON his business. He has brought in a new team member to work with clients two days per week and has increased his sales per client by at least 10%, having two price increases in twelve months, which all of his clients agreed with and some said "about time".

Adam's commitment and work rate to changing his business from time for money to a value added approach has been inspiring. He's also able to take what he has learnt about his own journey to further help his clients in their health challenges. Adding to his already knowledgeable and highly skilled mind.

Patrick and Sarah Tame

I first met Patrick just days after his business won the Most Effective Recruitment Marketing Campaign Award in the 2014 Recruiter Awards for Excellence. I'm not sure if the bottle of Bollinger I brought with me to congratulate Patrick was a factor but we started working together the following month.

Patrick got into recruitment after leaving the Army in 2003 and very quickly found his place in the world combining his fascination with business and love of people. A couple of years later and Patrick started his own recruitment firm growing from strength to strength.

At the time that we first met, Patrick was more interested in saving tax than anything else because he was, as he suspected, paying himself in a very tax inefficient way. But he also wanted to grow the business so it could run without him.

After describing how I would improve tax efficiency and going through the **PROFITS** Principles to show how we would create Patrick's ideal business running without him we quickly got to work.

Patrick had just got married to Sarah so it was perfect timing to re-structure the business and the way they pay themselves from the company.

After ticking the tax saving box we all worked together on creating a long term strategy plan for the business and agreed on the key steps that would need to happen to get there. This included systemisation, team recruitment and development, measuring the key metrics and improving them each month.

The hard work put in by Patrick, Sarah and their team is producing truly amazing results. We started working together in July 2014 and at the time of writing the business is ticking all of the boxes: Sales have increased by 22% to over £1m. Gross profit has increased by 50% and net profit has increased by 124%. Amazing result in such a short space of time!

Their team has doubled, a 100% increase, and the company net cash position has increased by 130%.

Patrick and Sarah's pay has only increased by 9% but the business and their take home pay is now more tax efficient than before, with tax saved of over £28,900.

Patrick and Sarah are now working less and less in the office. From Patrick working until 6pm every night he is now finishing at 3pm most days and some days if there is nothing to do he will leave even earlier. They return from holidays without hundreds of emails because they have all been taken care of while they were away. Visits to see clients in London haven't happened for over six months when they used to be a weekly occurrence. Recently Patrick took a week off on a whim and left the team to continue their great work without him.

Their quality of life has greatly improved while maintaining their high personal income from the business.

Patrick, a creative genius and natural leader, and Sarah, a grounded and thoughtful realist, are an inspiring duo with one complementing the other and they really deserve their success.

ACKNOWLEDGEMENTS

Without all the people in my life I would not be the person I am today and this book would not have been possible. I am grateful to everyone no matter how much time they have spent with me or how much help, tiny or huge, they have given me. I love and appreciate them all.

Most important my amazing, supportive and caring wife Natalie who is a hub of wise words. Our wonderful daughter Ella-Lily for her loving hugs and teaching me so much about myself through trying to become the father I want to be. I love you both and thank you.

My parents, Philip Goddard, Sue Briginshaw and Bob Briginshaw, my step father, for laying the foundations and teaching me so much. Thank you.

A special thank you to those who have helped me move out of my comfort zone, conquer limiting beliefs, to live in the present, be myself, see things with clarity and work towards my ideal life. Thank you, Adam Cox, Elvira Villarini and Eloise Ansell.

Thank you to my grandparents for their love, support and kindness. Thank you, Lillian and John Hind, Ella and Eric Goddard and Phyllis Briginshaw.

Thank you to my caring and selfless parents in-law, Julie and Jim O'Hara.

My brothers and sisters who each have a different and special place in my heart. Thank you, Robert, Rachel, Laine and Jon.

To my mentors and coaches, thank you for your wise words, powerful insights and challenging questions. Thank you, Steve Pipe, Mark Wickersham, Paul Dunn, Rob Say and AVN.

Thank you to the thought leaders who have inspired me to develop my own thoughts and to implement theirs. Thank you to Daniel Priestley, Roger James Hamilton, Sam Carpenter, Robert Kiyosaki,

Andrew Priestley, Scott Dinsmore and most importantly Michael E Gerber without whom I wouldn't have started this journey.

Thank you Darshana Ubl and Sonia Gill for helping me get my authentic message out there.

Thank you Lucy McCarraher and Joe Gregory for your skill and guidance to help bring this book to life.

I am also extremely grateful to the following people who have had a positive impact on my life: Kellie O'Hara, Neil Oakley, Ethan and Noah Oakley, Ryan Hall, John Moss, Michael and Chloe Moss, Nicola Briginshaw, Jordan Beasley, David Hind, John Briginshaw, Matthew Goddard, Mick Goddard, Dave and Lynne Goddard, Andy Goddard, John Print, David Barnes, Philip Nixon, Brian Maskell, Kevin Brodie-Farmer, Caroline Meredith, Rod Hamilton, Kim Deere, Lynne Greenmoor, Phil Ellerby, Rob Stafford, Jan McDermott, Jim Lockhart, Guy Robinson, Jane Fletcher, Sarah Cross, Tracy Clow, Neil McHugh, Claire Theobald, Stuart Harris, Tracy Harris, Graham Rossborough, Rachel Rossborough, Dan Taylor, Jayne Taylor, Steve King, Jane King, Guy James, Nicola James, Tom Taylor, Jo Taylor, Martin Norbury, Chris Waters, Sharon Dunne, Patrick Tame and Sarah Tame.

THE AUTHOR

Steven founded his first and second businesses in 2006 whilst still an employee as a chartered accountant, the first a bookkeeping business and the second an online affiliate business.

Learning from his mistakes, working with mentors and business owners since 2000, Steven was able to use that knowledge and experience to create his own chartered accountancy practice in 2012, build it to over six figures and sell it in 2015.

Now Steven spends his time on his passions: having fun, learning, creating, educating and inspiring that in others.

Steven does this via his role as COO and Founder of Clarity – an online global platform that helps accountants and business owners to build their ideal business.

He uses his own story, experience, knowledge and skill with his love of numbers and business to help fellow accountants and their clients get the time, money and freedom they deserve.

Steven has helped many accounting firm and business owners build towards their dream business. A start-up getting to over six figures in the first year; an over-worked fifty-hour per week 'job owner' getting to thirty-five hours per week with two days of those five working *on* his business; and taking a high six-figure business to well over seven figures with a net profit increase of 3043%.

Steven is working towards his legacy to bring entrepreneurship into primary and secondary schools, create an Entrepreneurs' University for anyone aged sixteen or over, who is already in business or not, to learn and build a lifestyle passion business that makes a difference; and to revolutionise the accountancy profession so all accountancy firms have a niche and a specialism to best serve the growing, and soon to be the norm, niched and specialised small global businesses.

Get in touch:
Web: www.stevenbriginshaw.com
Twitter: @SteveBriginshaw
Facebook: www.facebook.com/steven.briginshaw
YouTube: www.youtube.com/stevenbriginshaw

clarity.

Are you an accountant working with business owners?

If you want more profitable revenue, clients who want your business advisory services, and more time (with others delivering help to clients instead of you) then take the Success Factor quiz to get a tailored plan to achieve your goals...

https://hubs.la/H0GZb1c0

"Within just two weeks I had spoken to six clients and generated an additional £42,000 gross recurring revenue, at no extra cost!"
Graeme Tennick, Accountant

Are you a business owner who wants more help from your accountant?

If you want help to improve and grow your business, make better business decisions, and get the time, money and freedom you deserve then ask your accountant to take the Success Factor quiz to see how they can help you.

Send them this link to take the quiz...

https://hubs.la/H0GZb1c0

"I've never been so excited about my business! I now understand the numbers and have a plan to get the freedom I want."
Lucy Parsons